YEAR OF
YES
JOURNAL

SHONDA
RHIMES

SIMON & SCHUSTER

New York   London   Toronto   Sydney   New Delhi

Simon & Schuster
1230 Avenue of the Americas
New York, NY 10020

First Simon & Schuster hardcover edition December 2016

SIMON & SCHUSTER and colophon are registered
trademarks of Simon & Schuster, Inc.

For information about special discounts for bulk purchases,
please contact Simon & Schuster Special Sales at
1-866-506-1949 or business@simonandschuster.com.

The Simon & Schuster Speakers Bureau can bring authors to your live event.
For more information or to book an event, contact the
Simon & Schuster Speakers Bureau at 1-866-248-3049
or visit our website at www.simonspeakers.com.

Interior design by Ruth Lee-Mui

Manufactured in the United States of America

1   3   5   7   9   10   8   6   4   2

ISBN 978-1-5011-6305-0

INTRODUCTION

If you are holding this journal, I can only assume that you are maybe, perhaps *possibly,* thinking of starting your very own Year of Yes.

I like you already. We are already friends.

Hello, friend!

Not that long ago, I tried an experiment. I decided that for one year I would say YES. Not to *everything.* Not *yes* to jumping off a bridge or *yes* to quitting my job or *yes* to becoming a mail–order bride (eeeewww). Not even *yes* to all the fried chicken I could eat. Even though I really wanted to say *yes* to all the fried chicken I could eat, I didn't do it.

What I did do was this: I said *yes* to all the things that scared me, that took me out of my comfort zone, that had the ability to shake up my very small, very unsatisfying life. I thought it would be interesting. It turned out to be more than interesting. It turned out to be life changing.

I said *yes* as an experiment and ended up in the midst of a full-scale evolution. I *evolved*. Into a completely different person. A happier one. A healthier one. A more vocal one. Into ME. The me I had been afraid to allow to exist.

More than that? I started to actually *like* myself. Like, *like myself*. Think highly of . . . ME. I began to just enjoy the hell outta myself. Who knew that was possible? And I gotta tell you, liking yourself? Feels like Channing Tatum, Idris Elba and the whole cast of *Hamilton* wrapped in a bow for you on Christmas morning every single day.

(Sidenote: I do not condone stealing talented people and giving them as presents. But if they choose to come on their own, it's fine.)

ANYWAY, the point is: saying *yes* was revolutionary for me. So revolutionary that I wrote a book about it called, you guessed it, *Year of Yes*. So many of you have written to me and spoken to me about the book and how it has inspired you. I've been so grateful for that because, I'll be honest, I was a bit freaked out about the naked exposure of telling so much truth, about showing so much of my inner me to the world. And I think we all feel less alone when other people raise their hands to join the tribe and say, "Me too."

A lot of you awesome people said, *"ME TOO."* Bless you from your heads to your toes.

So I thought, maybe the best thing to do for those of you

in the tribe who also want Idris and Channing in your house singing with the cast of *Hamilton* on Christmas morning is this: create this Year of Yes journal to maybe make your Year of Yes a little bit easier.

How does it work? I'm glad you asked!

At the beginning of the journal—

—and that doesn't have to be the beginning of the year because I don't know about you but I suck at New Year's resolutions so it can just be a Tuesday in November if you want—

—anyway, at the beginning of the journal, you write down your goals. Your goals are things you are going to say *YES* to.

Your *YES* Goals.

Then (and this is where the seriously Cristina Yang intense student in me comes out) you can track and chart your *YES* Goals every single day in the journal.

Yes, honey, I said every day.

Or, you know, less if you are shaking your head and wondering what is wrong with me.

Then you do some checking and reassessing at the six-month and one-year mark for each *YES* Goal. Meaning you have to be accountable for how your *YES* Goals are going.

That is right. Go all up into your journal and JUDGE yourself. Don't let anybody else judge you. But DO judge yourself. Hold yourself accountable. Look at yourself. Look at all your gooey places. Look at the ugly places. Look at the places you hope nobody sees. Those are the places you need to a) start loving and b) start trying to yank right out into the light. (Unless, you know, you should be covering those places with a pair of panties. Then . . . nevermind.) The point is: if you feel uncomfortable but want to change or wish you were braver, dive in. Dive right in and start swimming.

Across the sea of insecurity is a whole beach full of happy people who don't care how they look in bikinis.

Above all, this journal should be used however you please. It's yours. It belongs to you. That means you make all the rules. The only rule that comes with this journal? Is that you say YES.

I wish you a lifetime of change.

Enjoy.

Your friend,
Shonda

What is my vision for myself this year? Who do I want to be?

_____

_____

_____

_____

_____

_____

_____

_____

_____

_____

_____

_____

_____

_____

_____

_____

_____

_____

_____

_____

_____

_____

_____

_____

_____

What do I want to say YES to?

_____
_____
_____
_____
_____
_____
_____
_____
_____
_____
_____
_____
_____
_____
_____
_____
_____
_____
_____
_____
_____
_____
_____
_____
_____
_____
_____
_____
_____
_____

What do you hope to change about yourself in this Year of Yes?

_____

_____

_____

_____

_____

_____

_____

_____

_____

_____

_____

_____

_____

_____

_____

_____

_____

_____

_____

_____

_____

_____

_____

_____

_____

Six startling words:

YOU

NEVER SAY

YES

TO ANYTHING.

That's my truth.

 WHAT'S YOURS?

MONTH ONE

YES TO BEAUTIFUL

I am not interested in simply accepting myself for who I am. That's basic existence. I want to ENJOY who I am. I'm delightful, I'm gorgeous, I'm EVERYTHING. You are too.

Things I will say YES to this month:

_____
_____
_____
_____
_____
_____
_____
_____
_____
_____
_____
_____
_____

Beautiful

DAY 1

The YESes I handled today:

_____

_____

_____

_____

_____

_____

_____

What I gained by saying YES:

_____

_____

_____

_____

_____

_____

_____

What were the dark and twisty parts of today's YESes?

_____

_____

_____

_____

_____

_____

_____

Beautiful

DAY 2

The YESes I handled today:

_____

_____

_____

_____

_____

_____

What I gained by saying YES:

_____

_____

_____

_____

_____

_____

What were the dark and twisty parts of today's YESes?

_____

_____

_____

_____

_____

_____

Beautiful

DAY 3

The YESes I handled today:

_____

_____

_____

_____

_____

_____

_____

What I gained by saying YES:

_____

_____

_____

_____

_____

_____

What were the dark and twisty parts of today's YESes?

_____

_____

_____

_____

_____

_____

Beautiful

DAY 4

The YESes I handled today:

_____
_____
_____
_____
_____
_____
_____

What I gained by saying YES:

_____
_____
_____
_____
_____
_____

What were the dark and twisty parts of today's YESes?

_____
_____
_____
_____
_____
_____

Beautiful

DAY 5

The YESes I handled today:

_____

_____

_____

_____

_____

_____

What I gained by saying YES:

_____

_____

_____

_____

_____

_____

What were the dark and twisty parts of today's YESes?

_____

_____

_____

_____

_____

_____

Beautiful

DAY 6

The YESes I handled today:

_____
_____
_____
_____
_____
_____
_____

What I gained by saying YES:

_____
_____
_____
_____
_____
_____
_____

What were the dark and twisty parts of today's YESes?

_____
_____
_____
_____
_____
_____
_____

Beautiful

DAY 7

The YESes I handled today:

_____

_____

_____

_____

_____

_____

What I gained by saying YES:

_____

_____

_____

_____

_____

_____

What were the dark and twisty parts of today's YESes?

_____

_____

_____

_____

_____

_____

Beautiful

DAY 8

The YESes I handled today:

_____

_____

_____

_____

_____

_____

_____

What I gained by saying YES:

_____

_____

_____

_____

_____

_____

_____

What were the dark and twisty parts of today's YESes?

_____

_____

_____

_____

_____

_____

_____

Beautiful

DAY 9

The YESes I handled today:

_____
_____
_____
_____
_____
_____
_____

What I gained by saying YES:

_____
_____
_____
_____
_____
_____
_____

What were the dark and twisty parts of today's YESes?

_____
_____
_____
_____
_____
_____
_____

IT'S OKAY

———— · ————

to want to

BE
SEEN.

———— · ————

It's okay to

like being

 SEEN.

———— · ————

Beautiful

DAY 10

The YESes I handled today:

_____

_____

_____

_____

_____

_____

What I gained by saying YES:

_____

_____

_____

_____

_____

_____

What were the dark and twisty parts of today's YESes?

_____

_____

_____

_____

_____

_____

Beautiful

DAY 11

The YESes I handled today:

_____
_____
_____
_____
_____
_____
_____

What I gained by saying YES:

_____
_____
_____
_____
_____
_____
_____

What were the dark and twisty parts of today's YESes?

_____
_____
_____
_____
_____
_____
_____

Beautiful

DAY 12

The YESes I handled today:

_____
_____
_____
_____
_____
_____

What I gained by saying YES:

_____
_____
_____
_____
_____
_____

What were the dark and twisty parts of today's YESes?

_____
_____
_____
_____
_____
_____

Beautiful

DAY 13

The YESes I handled today:

_____

_____

_____

_____

_____

_____

What I gained by saying YES:

_____

_____

_____

_____

_____

_____

What were the dark and twisty parts of today's YESes?

_____

_____

_____

_____

_____

_____

Beautiful

DAY 14

The YESes I handled today:

_____

_____

_____

_____

_____

_____

_____

What I gained by saying YES:

_____

_____

_____

_____

_____

_____

_____

What were the dark and twisty parts of today's YESes?

_____

_____

_____

_____

_____

_____

_____

Beautiful

What am I unhappy with?

_____

_____

_____

_____

_____

_____

_____

_____

_____

_____

What do I love about myself?

_____

_____

_____

_____

_____

_____

_____

_____

_____

_____

Beautiful

DAY 15

The YESes I handled today:

_____
_____
_____
_____
_____
_____
_____

What I gained by saying YES:

_____
_____
_____
_____
_____
_____
_____

What were the dark and twisty parts of today's YESes?

_____
_____
_____
_____
_____
_____
_____

Beautiful

DAY 16

The YESes I handled today:

_____
_____
_____
_____
_____
_____
_____

What I gained by saying YES:

_____
_____
_____
_____
_____
_____
_____

What were the dark and twisty parts of today's YESes?

_____
_____
_____
_____
_____
_____
_____

Beautiful

DAY 17

The YESes I handled today:

_____

_____

_____

_____

_____

_____

_____

What I gained by saying YES:

_____

_____

_____

_____

_____

_____

_____

What were the dark and twisty parts of today's YESes?

_____

_____

_____

_____

_____

_____

_____

Beautiful

DAY 18

The YESes I handled today:

_____
_____
_____
_____
_____
_____

What I gained by saying YES:

_____
_____
_____
_____
_____
_____

What were the dark and twisty parts of today's YESes?

_____
_____
_____
_____
_____
_____

Beautiful

DAY 19

The YESes I handled today:

_____
_____
_____
_____
_____
_____
_____

What I gained by saying YES:

_____
_____
_____
_____
_____
_____
_____

What were the dark and twisty parts of today's YESes?

_____
_____
_____
_____
_____
_____

SAYING

YES

IS

COURAGE.

Beautiful

DAY 20

The YESes I handled today:

_____
_____
_____
_____
_____
_____
_____

What I gained by saying YES:

_____
_____
_____
_____
_____
_____
_____

What were the dark and twisty parts of today's YESes?

_____
_____
_____
_____
_____
_____

Beautiful

DAY 21

The YESes I handled today:

_____

_____

_____

_____

_____

_____

_____

What I gained by saying YES:

_____

_____

_____

_____

_____

_____

_____

What were the dark and twisty parts of today's YESes?

_____

_____

_____

_____

_____

_____

_____

Beautiful

DAY 22

The YESes I handled today:

_____

_____

_____

_____

_____

_____

_____

What I gained by saying YES:

_____

_____

_____

_____

_____

_____

_____

What were the dark and twisty parts of today's YESes?

_____

_____

_____

_____

_____

_____

_____

Beautiful

DAY 23

The YESes I handled today:

_____

_____

_____

_____

_____

_____

What I gained by saying YES:

_____

_____

_____

_____

_____

_____

What were the dark and twisty parts of today's YESes?

_____

_____

_____

_____

_____

_____

Beautiful

DAY 24

The YESes I handled today:

_____
_____
_____
_____
_____
_____
_____

What I gained by saying YES:

_____
_____
_____
_____
_____
_____
_____

What were the dark and twisty parts of today's YESes?

_____
_____
_____
_____
_____
_____
_____

Beautiful

DAY 25

The YESes I handled today:

_____
_____
_____
_____
_____
_____
_____

What I gained by saying YES:

_____
_____
_____
_____
_____
_____

What were the dark and twisty parts of today's YESes?

_____
_____
_____
_____
_____
_____
_____

Beautiful

DAY 26

The YESes I handled today:

_____
_____
_____
_____
_____
_____
_____
_____

What I gained by saying YES:

_____
_____
_____
_____
_____
_____
_____

What were the dark and twisty parts of today's YESes?

_____
_____
_____
_____
_____
_____

Beautiful

DAY 27

The YESes I handled today:

_____

_____

_____

_____

_____

_____

_____

What I gained by saying YES:

_____

_____

_____

_____

_____

_____

_____

What were the dark and twisty parts of today's YESes?

_____

_____

_____

_____

_____

_____

_____

Beautiful

DAY 28

The YESes I handled today:

_____
_____
_____
_____
_____
_____
_____

What I gained by saying YES:

_____
_____
_____
_____
_____
_____
_____

What were the dark and twisty parts of today's YESes?

_____
_____
_____
_____
_____
_____
_____

Beautiful

DAY 29

The YESes I handled today:

_____

_____

_____

_____

_____

_____

What I gained by saying YES:

_____

_____

_____

_____

_____

_____

What were the dark and twisty parts of today's YESes?

_____

_____

_____

_____

_____

_____

Beautiful

DAY 30

The YESes I handled today:

_____
_____
_____
_____
_____
_____
_____

What I gained by saying YES:

_____
_____
_____
_____
_____
_____
_____

What were the dark and twisty parts of today's YESes?

_____
_____
_____
_____
_____
_____

Beautiful

DAY 31

The YESes I handled today:

_____

_____

_____

_____

_____

_____

_____

What I gained by saying YES:

_____

_____

_____

_____

_____

_____

_____

What were the dark and twisty parts of today's YESes?

_____

_____

_____

_____

_____

_____

_____

MONTH TWO

YES TO DOING

Be a doer not a dreamer.

Things I will say YES to this month:

_____

_____

_____

_____

_____

_____

_____

_____

_____

_____

_____

_____

_____

_____

_____

_____

Doing

Six Things to Do for Inspiration

1. Find a song that makes you feel powerful and sing it in the shower. For me, that's Beyoncé. ANY Beyoncé. For you, it could be something different.

2. Get a mentor. And by that, I don't mean a real-life mentor. You don't "get" one of those. Those . . . just grow from relationships you have. I mean, find someone out there whose words of wisdom make you feel stronger. Oprah. Sheryl Sandberg. Maya. Mrs. Obama. Indira Gandhi, Gloria Steinem or one of the all-time greats, Eleanor Roosevelt. Eleanor had the answer to absolutely everything.

3. Read a book that makes you wanna get off the couch: all of the Harry Potters because Hermione is everything; anything by Alice Walker because, please; Anne Lamott reminds you that nothing is insurmountable; Octavia Butler reminds you that everything is possible.

4. Stop looking in the mirror. I'm serious. For a day. For a week. Ignore that reflection staring back at you that requires you to judge yourself. Just . . . turn your back on it. Give yourself the option of letting your only reflection be what you accomplish and how you touch another person's life.

5. Just do one thing. Just one. It can be small. It only needs to be different from what you usually do. Break your normal pattern. Drink tea instead of coffee. Say hello to everyone you see. Walk instead of drive. Eat lunch in the park instead of at your desk. Smile at people. Speak up. Meet up with a friend to hang out instead of watching TV alone. Just do ONE thing. Step off your normal path. And see where it leads you.

And if you can't manage to do any of those?

6. Get dressed. I'm serious. Take a shower. Get clean. And get dressed. It is amazing how your brain starts to hum when you are wearing a clean pair of underwear. In clean panties, anything is possible.

DITCH

the

DREAM.

BE A

DOER,

not a dreamer.

Doing

DAY 1

The YESes I handled today:

_____

_____

_____

_____

_____

_____

_____

What I gained by saying YES:

_____

_____

_____

_____

_____

_____

_____

What were the dark and twisty parts of today's YESes?

_____

_____

_____

_____

_____

_____

_____

Doing

DAY 2

The YESes I handled today:

_____
_____
_____
_____
_____
_____

What I gained by saying YES:

_____
_____
_____
_____
_____
_____

What were the dark and twisty parts of today's YESes?

_____
_____
_____
_____
_____
_____

Doing

DAY 3

The YESes I handled today:

_____
_____
_____
_____
_____
_____
_____

What I gained by saying YES:

_____
_____
_____
_____
_____
_____
_____

What were the dark and twisty parts of today's YESes?

_____
_____
_____
_____
_____
_____
_____

DAY 4

The YESes I handled today:

_____

_____

_____

_____

_____

_____

_____

What I gained by saying YES:

_____

_____

_____

_____

_____

_____

_____

What were the dark and twisty parts of today's YESes?

_____

_____

_____

_____

_____

_____

_____

Doing

DAY 5

The YESes I handled today:

_____

_____

_____

_____

_____

_____

_____

What I gained by saying YES:

_____

_____

_____

_____

_____

_____

_____

What were the dark and twisty parts of today's YESes?

_____

_____

_____

_____

_____

_____

_____

Doing

DAY 6

The YESes I handled today:

_____

_____

_____

_____

_____

_____

What I gained by saying YES:

_____

_____

_____

_____

_____

_____

What were the dark and twisty parts of today's YESes?

_____

_____

_____

_____

_____

_____

Doing

DAY 7

The YESes I handled today:

_____
_____
_____
_____
_____
_____
_____

What I gained by saying YES:

_____
_____
_____
_____
_____
_____
_____

What were the dark and twisty parts of today's YESes?

_____
_____
_____
_____
_____
_____
_____

Doing

DAY 8

The YESes I handled today:

_____

_____

_____

_____

_____

_____

_____

What I gained by saying YES:

_____

_____

_____

_____

_____

_____

_____

What were the dark and twisty parts of today's YESes?

_____

_____

_____

_____

_____

_____

_____

Doing

DAY 9

The YESes I handled today:

_____

_____

_____

_____

_____

_____

_____

What I gained by saying YES:

_____

_____

_____

_____

_____

_____

_____

What were the dark and twisty parts of today's YESes?

_____

_____

_____

_____

_____

_____

_____

Doing

DAY 10

The YESes I handled today:

_____

_____

_____

_____

_____

_____

_____

What I gained by saying YES:

_____

_____

_____

_____

_____

_____

_____

What were the dark and twisty parts of today's YESes?

_____

_____

_____

_____

_____

_____

_____

YES

should feel

like

THE

SUN.

Doing

DAY 11

The YESes I handled today:

_____

_____

_____

_____

_____

_____

_____

What I gained by saying YES:

_____

_____

_____

_____

_____

_____

What were the dark and twisty parts of today's YESes?

_____

_____

_____

_____

_____

_____

Doing

DAY 12

The YESes I handled today:

_____

_____

_____

_____

_____

_____

_____

What I gained by saying YES:

_____

_____

_____

_____

_____

_____

_____

What were the dark and twisty parts of today's YESes?

_____

_____

_____

_____

_____

_____

_____

Doing

DAY 13

The YESes I handled today:

_____

_____

_____

_____

_____

_____

_____

What I gained by saying YES:

_____

_____

_____

_____

_____

_____

_____

What were the dark and twisty parts of today's YESes?

_____

_____

_____

_____

_____

_____

_____

Doing

DAY 14

The YESes I handled today:

_____

_____

_____

_____

_____

_____

_____

What I gained by saying YES:

_____

_____

_____

_____

_____

_____

_____

What were the dark and twisty parts of today's YESes?

_____

_____

_____

_____

_____

_____

_____

Doing

What motivates you to pursue your goals?

_____
_____
_____
_____
_____
_____
_____
_____
_____
_____
_____
_____
_____
_____
_____
_____
_____
_____
_____
_____
_____
_____
_____
_____
_____
_____
_____

Doing

DAY 15

The YESes I handled today:

_____

_____

_____

_____

_____

_____

_____

What I gained by saying YES:

_____

_____

_____

_____

_____

_____

_____

What were the dark and twisty parts of today's YESes?

_____

_____

_____

_____

_____

_____

_____

Doing

DAY 16

The YESes I handled today:

_____
_____
_____
_____
_____
_____
_____

What I gained by saying YES:

_____
_____
_____
_____
_____
_____
_____

What were the dark and twisty parts of today's YESes?

_____
_____
_____
_____
_____
_____
_____

Doing

DAY 17

The YESes I handled today:

_____

_____

_____

_____

_____

_____

_____

What I gained by saying YES:

_____

_____

_____

_____

_____

_____

_____

What were the dark and twisty parts of today's YESes?

_____

_____

_____

_____

_____

_____

Doing

DAY 18

The YESes I handled today:

_____

_____

_____

_____

_____

_____

_____

What I gained by saying YES:

_____

_____

_____

_____

_____

_____

_____

What were the dark and twisty parts of today's YESes?

_____

_____

_____

_____

_____

_____

_____

_____

Doing

DAY 19

The YESes I handled today:

_____
_____
_____
_____
_____
_____

What I gained by saying YES:

_____
_____
_____
_____
_____
_____

What were the dark and twisty parts of today's YESes?

_____
_____
_____
_____
_____
_____

Doing

DAY 20

The YESes I handled today:

_____

_____

_____

_____

_____

_____

_____

What I gained by saying YES:

_____

_____

_____

_____

_____

_____

_____

What were the dark and twisty parts of today's YESes?

_____

_____

_____

_____

_____

_____

_____

Doing

DAY 21

The YESes I handled today:

_____

_____

_____

_____

_____

_____

_____

What I gained by saying YES:

_____

_____

_____

_____

_____

_____

What were the dark and twisty parts of today's YESes?

_____

_____

_____

_____

_____

_____

_____

DREAMS

do not come true

JUST BECAUSE

you dream them.

IT'S HARD WORK

that

MAKES THINGS HAPPEN.

IT'S HARD WORK

that

CREATES CHANGE.

Doing

DAY 22

The YESes I handled today:

_____
_____
_____
_____
_____
_____
_____

What I gained by saying YES:

_____
_____
_____
_____
_____
_____
_____

What were the dark and twisty parts of today's YESes?

_____
_____
_____
_____
_____
_____
_____

Doing

DAY 23

The YESes I handled today:

_____
_____
_____
_____
_____
_____
_____
_____

What I gained by saying YES:

_____
_____
_____
_____
_____
_____
_____
_____

What were the dark and twisty parts of today's YESes?

_____
_____
_____
_____
_____
_____
_____
_____

Doing

DAY 24

The YESes I handled today:

_____
_____
_____
_____
_____
_____
_____

What I gained by saying YES:

_____
_____
_____
_____
_____
_____
_____

What were the dark and twisty parts of today's YESes?

_____
_____
_____
_____
_____
_____
_____

Doing

DAY 25

The YESes I handled today:

_____
_____
_____
_____
_____
_____
_____

What I gained by saying YES:

_____
_____
_____
_____
_____
_____
_____

What were the dark and twisty parts of today's YESes?

_____
_____
_____
_____
_____
_____
_____

Doing

DAY 26

The YESes I handled today:

_____
_____
_____
_____
_____
_____
_____

What I gained by saying YES:

_____
_____
_____
_____
_____
_____

What were the dark and twisty parts of today's YESes?

_____
_____
_____
_____
_____
_____
_____

Doing

DAY 27

The YESes I handled today:

_____
_____
_____
_____
_____
_____
_____

What I gained by saying YES:

_____
_____
_____
_____
_____
_____
_____

What were the dark and twisty parts of today's YESes?

_____
_____
_____
_____
_____
_____
_____

DON'T

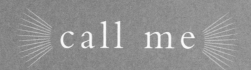 call me

LUCKY.

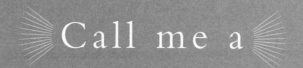 Call me a

BADASS.

Doing

DAY 28

The YESes I handled today:

_____
_____
_____
_____
_____
_____

What I gained by saying YES:

_____
_____
_____
_____
_____
_____

What were the dark and twisty parts of today's YESes?

_____
_____
_____
_____
_____
_____

Doing

DAY 29

The YESes I handled today:

_____
_____
_____
_____
_____
_____
_____

What I gained by saying YES:

_____
_____
_____
_____
_____
_____
_____

What were the dark and twisty parts of today's YESes?

_____
_____
_____
_____
_____
_____
_____

Doing

DAY 30

The YESes I handled today:

_____
_____
_____
_____
_____
_____
_____

What I gained by saying YES:

_____
_____
_____
_____
_____
_____
_____

What were the dark and twisty parts of today's YESes?

_____
_____
_____
_____
_____
_____
_____

DAY 31

The YESes I handled today:

_____

_____

_____

_____

_____

_____

_____

What I gained by saying YES:

_____

_____

_____

_____

_____

_____

_____

What were the dark and twisty parts of today's YESes?

_____

_____

_____

_____

_____

_____

_____

MONTH THREE

YES TO PLAY

We are raised to work hard. To strive for greatness.
To achieve. But when did we forget how to play?
Without time to recharge and relax, how long will we
succeed at work? And how much fun will work be?

Things I will say YES to this month:

_____

_____

_____

_____

_____

_____

_____

_____

_____

_____

_____

_____

Play

Play requires other people. What are some social activities you want to try this month?

_____

_____

_____

_____

_____

_____

_____

_____

_____

_____

_____

_____

_____

_____

_____

_____

_____

_____

_____

_____

_____

_____

_____

_____

_____

_____

YOU

···· have a ····

BUSY

LIFE.

——— But you ———

CAN PLAY

 for

FIFTEEN

MINUTES.

Play

DAY 1

The YESes I handled today:

_____
_____
_____
_____
_____
_____
_____

What I gained by saying YES:

_____
_____
_____
_____
_____
_____
_____

What were the dark and twisty parts of today's YESes?

_____
_____
_____
_____
_____
_____
_____

Play

DAY 2

The YESes I handled today:

_____
_____
_____
_____
_____
_____
_____

What I gained by saying YES:

_____
_____
_____
_____
_____
_____

What were the dark and twisty parts of today's YESes?

_____
_____
_____
_____
_____
_____

DAY 3

The YESes I handled today:

_____

_____

_____

_____

_____

_____

_____

What I gained by saying YES:

_____

_____

_____

_____

_____

_____

_____

What were the dark and twisty parts of today's YESes?

_____

_____

_____

_____

_____

_____

_____

Play

DAY 4

The YESes I handled today:

_____

_____

_____

_____

_____

_____

_____

What I gained by saying YES:

_____

_____

_____

_____

_____

_____

_____

What were the dark and twisty parts of today's YESes?

_____

_____

_____

_____

_____

_____

_____

Play

DAY 5

The YESes I handled today:

_____

_____

_____

_____

_____

_____

_____

What I gained by saying YES:

_____

_____

_____

_____

_____

_____

What were the dark and twisty parts of today's YESes?

_____

_____

_____

_____

_____

_____

Play

DAY 6

The YESes I handled today:

_____

_____

_____

_____

_____

_____

_____

What I gained by saying YES:

_____

_____

_____

_____

_____

_____

_____

What were the dark and twisty parts of today's YESes?

_____

_____

_____

_____

_____

_____

_____

Play

DAY 7

The YESes I handled today:

_____

_____

_____

_____

_____

_____

_____

What I gained by saying YES:

_____

_____

_____

_____

_____

_____

_____

What were the dark and twisty parts of today's YESes?

_____

_____

_____

_____

_____

_____

_____

Play

DAY 8

The YESes I handled today:

_____

_____

_____

_____

_____

_____

_____

What I gained by saying YES:

_____

_____

_____

_____

_____

_____

_____

What were the dark and twisty parts of today's YESes?

_____

_____

_____

_____

_____

_____

_____

Play

DAY 9

The YESes I handled today:

_____
_____
_____
_____
_____
_____
_____

What I gained by saying YES:

_____
_____
_____
_____
_____
_____
_____

What were the dark and twisty parts of today's YESes?

_____
_____
_____
_____
_____
_____
_____

Play

DAY 10

The YESes I handled today:

_____

_____

_____

_____

_____

_____

_____

What I gained by saying YES:

_____

_____

_____

_____

_____

_____

_____

What were the dark and twisty parts of today's YESes?

_____

_____

_____

_____

_____

_____

_____

Play

DAY 11

The YESes I handled today:

_____
_____
_____
_____
_____
_____
_____

What I gained by saying YES:

_____
_____
_____
_____
_____
_____
_____

What were the dark and twisty parts of today's YESes?

_____
_____
_____
_____
_____
_____

Play

DAY 12

The YESes I handled today:

_____

_____

_____

_____

_____

_____

_____

What I gained by saying YES:

_____

_____

_____

_____

_____

_____

_____

What were the dark and twisty parts of today's YESes?

_____

_____

_____

_____

_____

_____

_____

Play

DAY 13

The YESes I handled today:

_____
_____
_____
_____
_____
_____

What I gained by saying YES:

_____
_____
_____
_____
_____
_____

What were the dark and twisty parts of today's YESes?

_____
_____
_____
_____
_____
_____

Play

DAY 14

The YESes I handled today:

_____
_____
_____
_____
_____
_____

What I gained by saying YES:

_____
_____
_____
_____
_____
_____

What were the dark and twisty parts of today's YESes?

_____
_____
_____
_____
_____
_____

Play

DAY 15

The YESes I handled today:

_____
_____
_____
_____
_____
_____
_____

What I gained by saying YES:

_____
_____
_____
_____
_____
_____

What were the dark and twisty parts of today's YESes?

_____
_____
_____
_____
_____
_____

Wanna

PLAY?

YES.

DAY 16

The YESes I handled today:

_____

_____

_____

_____

_____

_____

_____

What I gained by saying YES:

_____

_____

_____

_____

_____

_____

_____

What were the dark and twisty parts of today's YESes?

_____

_____

_____

_____

_____

_____

_____

Play

DAY 17

The YESes I handled today:

_____

_____

_____

_____

_____

_____

What I gained by saying YES:

_____

_____

_____

_____

_____

_____

What were the dark and twisty parts of today's YESes?

_____

_____

_____

_____

_____

_____

_____

Play

DAY 18

The YESes I handled today:

_____
_____
_____
_____
_____
_____
_____

What I gained by saying YES:

_____
_____
_____
_____
_____
_____

What were the dark and twisty parts of today's YESes?

_____
_____
_____
_____
_____
_____
_____

Play

DAY 19

The YESes I handled today:

_____

_____

_____

_____

_____

_____

_____

What I gained by saying YES:

_____

_____

_____

_____

_____

_____

_____

What were the dark and twisty parts of today's YESes?

_____

_____

_____

_____

_____

_____

_____

MONTH THREE

Play

DAY 20

The YESes I handled today:

_____
_____
_____
_____
_____
_____
_____

What I gained by saying YES:

_____
_____
_____
_____
_____
_____
_____

What were the dark and twisty parts of today's YESes?

_____
_____
_____
_____
_____
_____
_____

Play

DAY 21

The YESes I handled today:

_____
_____
_____
_____
_____
_____
_____

What I gained by saying YES:

_____
_____
_____
_____
_____
_____
_____

What were the dark and twisty parts of today's YESes?

_____
_____
_____
_____
_____
_____
_____

Play

DAY 22

The YESes I handled today:

_____

_____

_____

_____

_____

_____

What I gained by saying YES:

_____

_____

_____

_____

_____

_____

What were the dark and twisty parts of today's YESes?

_____

_____

_____

_____

_____

_____

_____

Play

DAY 23

The YESes I handled today:

_____
_____
_____
_____
_____
_____
_____

What I gained by saying YES:

_____
_____
_____
_____
_____
_____
_____

What were the dark and twisty parts of today's YESes?

_____
_____
_____
_____
_____
_____
_____

Play

DAY 24

The YESes I handled today:

_____
_____
_____
_____
_____
_____
_____

What I gained by saying YES:

_____
_____
_____
_____
_____
_____
_____

What were the dark and twisty parts of today's YESes?

_____
_____
_____
_____
_____
_____
_____

Play

DAY 25

The YESes I handled today:

_____

_____

_____

_____

_____

_____

_____

What I gained by saying YES:

_____

_____

_____

_____

_____

_____

_____

What were the dark and twisty parts of today's YESes?

_____

_____

_____

_____

_____

_____

_____

Play

DAY 26

The YESes I handled today:

_____

_____

_____

_____

_____

_____

_____

What I gained by saying YES:

_____

_____

_____

_____

_____

_____

_____

What were the dark and twisty parts of today's YESes?

_____

_____

_____

_____

_____

_____

Play

DAY 27

The YESes I handled today:

_____

_____

_____

_____

_____

_____

_____

What I gained by saying YES:

_____

_____

_____

_____

_____

_____

_____

What were the dark and twisty parts of today's YESes?

_____

_____

_____

_____

_____

_____

_____

Play

DAY 28

The YESes I handled today:

_____

_____

_____

_____

_____

_____

_____

What I gained by saying YES:

_____

_____

_____

_____

_____

_____

What were the dark and twisty parts of today's YESes?

_____

_____

_____

_____

_____

_____

Play

DAY 29

The YESes I handled today:

_____
_____
_____
_____
_____
_____
_____

What I gained by saying YES:

_____
_____
_____
_____
_____
_____
_____

What were the dark and twisty parts of today's YESes?

_____
_____
_____
_____
_____
_____

Play

DAY 30

The YESes I handled today:

_____
_____
_____
_____
_____
_____
_____

What I gained by saying YES:

_____
_____
_____
_____
_____
_____
_____

What were the dark and twisty parts of today's YESes?

_____
_____
_____
_____
_____
_____
_____

Play

DAY 31

The YESes I handled today:

_____

_____

_____

_____

_____

_____

_____

What I gained by saying YES:

_____

_____

_____

_____

_____

_____

_____

What were the dark and twisty parts of today's YESes?

_____

_____

_____

_____

_____

_____

_____

Body

MONTH FOUR

YES TO MY BODY

Your body is priceless. Stop hating it. It deserves your love,
safekeeping and respect. Keep it healthy, keep it protected and
only share it with those who know how to appreciate it.
Don't make me tell you twice.

Things I will say YES to this month:

_____
_____
_____
_____
_____
_____
_____
_____
_____
_____
_____
_____

Body

Go stand in the mirror. List three things you love about yourself today:

_____

_____

_____

_____

_____

_____

_____

_____

_____

_____

_____

_____

_____

_____

_____

_____

_____

_____

_____

_____

_____

_____

_____

_____

_____

_____

ALWAYS

— a —

WORK

— in —

PROGRESS.

Body

DAY 1

The YESes I handled today:

_____
_____
_____
_____
_____
_____
_____

What I gained by saying YES:

_____
_____
_____
_____
_____
_____
_____

What were the dark and twisty parts of today's YESes?

_____
_____
_____
_____
_____
_____
_____

Body

DAY 2

The YESes I handled today:

_____
_____
_____
_____
_____
_____
_____

What I gained by saying YES:

_____
_____
_____
_____
_____
_____
_____

What were the dark and twisty parts of today's YESes?

_____
_____
_____
_____
_____
_____
_____

Body

DAY 3

The YESes I handled today:

_____
_____
_____
_____
_____
_____
_____

What I gained by saying YES:

_____
_____
_____
_____
_____
_____
_____

What were the dark and twisty parts of today's YESes?

_____
_____
_____
_____
_____
_____
_____

Body

DAY 4

The YESes I handled today:

_____
_____
_____
_____
_____
_____
_____

What I gained by saying YES:

_____
_____
_____
_____
_____
_____
_____

What were the dark and twisty parts of today's YESes?

_____
_____
_____
_____
_____
_____

Body

DAY 5

The YESes I handled today:

_____
_____
_____
_____
_____
_____
_____

What I gained by saying YES:

_____
_____
_____
_____
_____
_____
_____

What were the dark and twisty parts of today's YESes?

_____
_____
_____
_____
_____
_____
_____

Body

DAY 6

The YESes I handled today:

_____
_____
_____
_____
_____
_____
_____

What I gained by saying YES:

_____
_____
_____
_____
_____
_____
_____

What were the dark and twisty parts of today's YESes?

_____
_____
_____
_____
_____
_____
_____

Body

DAY 7

The YESes I handled today:

_____
_____
_____
_____
_____
_____
_____

What I gained by saying YES:

_____
_____
_____
_____
_____
_____
_____

What were the dark and twisty parts of today's YESes?

_____
_____
_____
_____
_____
_____
_____

Body

What are some things I can do better to care for my body this month?

_____
_____
_____
_____
_____
_____
_____
_____
_____
_____
_____
_____
_____
_____
_____
_____
_____
_____
_____
_____
_____
_____
_____
_____
_____
_____
_____
_____

Body

DAY 8

The YESes I handled today:

_____

_____

_____

_____

_____

_____

What I gained by saying YES:

_____

_____

_____

_____

_____

_____

What were the dark and twisty parts of today's YESes?

_____

_____

_____

_____

_____

_____

_____

Body

DAY 9

The YESes I handled today:

_____
_____
_____
_____
_____
_____
_____

What I gained by saying YES:

_____
_____
_____
_____
_____
_____
_____

What were the dark and twisty parts of today's YESes?

_____
_____
_____
_____
_____
_____
_____

Body

DAY 10

The YESes I handled today:

_____
_____
_____
_____
_____
_____
_____

What I gained by saying YES:

_____
_____
_____
_____
_____
_____
_____

What were the dark and twisty parts of today's YESes?

_____
_____
_____
_____
_____
_____
_____

Body

DAY 11

The YESes I handled today:

_____
_____
_____
_____
_____
_____
_____

What I gained by saying YES:

_____
_____
_____
_____
_____
_____

What were the dark and twisty parts of today's YESes?

_____
_____
_____
_____
_____
_____
_____

Body

DAY 12

The YESes I handled today:

_____

_____

_____

_____

_____

_____

_____

What I gained by saying YES:

_____

_____

_____

_____

_____

_____

_____

What were the dark and twisty parts of today's YESes?

_____

_____

_____

_____

_____

_____

_____

Body

DAY 13

The YESes I handled today:

_____

_____

_____

_____

_____

_____

_____

What I gained by saying YES:

_____

_____

_____

_____

_____

_____

_____

What were the dark and twisty parts of today's YESes?

_____

_____

_____

_____

_____

_____

_____

DAY 14

The YESes I handled today:

_____

_____

_____

_____

_____

_____

_____

What I gained by saying YES:

_____

_____

_____

_____

_____

_____

_____

What were the dark and twisty parts of today's YESes?

_____

_____

_____

_____

_____

_____

_____

Body

DAY 15

The YESes I handled today:

_____

_____

_____

_____

_____

_____

_____

What I gained by saying YES:

_____

_____

_____

_____

_____

_____

_____

What were the dark and twisty parts of today's YESes?

_____

_____

_____

_____

_____

_____

_____

Body

DAY 16

The YESes I handled today:

_____
_____
_____
_____
_____
_____
_____

What I gained by saying YES:

_____
_____
_____
_____
_____
_____
_____

What were the dark and twisty parts of today's YESes?

_____
_____
_____
_____
_____
_____
_____

Body

DAY 17

The YESes I handled today:

_____

_____

_____

_____

_____

_____

_____

What I gained by saying YES:

_____

_____

_____

_____

_____

_____

What were the dark and twisty parts of today's YESes?

_____

_____

_____

_____

_____

_____

_____

Body

DAY 18

The YESes I handled today:

_____

_____

_____

_____

_____

_____

_____

What I gained by saying YES:

_____

_____

_____

_____

_____

_____

What were the dark and twisty parts of today's YESes?

_____

_____

_____

_____

_____

_____

DAY 19

The YESes I handled today:

_____
_____
_____
_____
_____
_____
_____

What I gained by saying YES:

_____
_____
_____
_____
_____
_____
_____

What were the dark and twisty parts of today's YESes?

_____
_____
_____
_____
_____
_____
_____

This is

WHO

I

AM.

Body

DAY 20

The YESes I handled today:

_____

_____

_____

_____

_____

_____

_____

What I gained by saying YES:

_____

_____

_____

_____

_____

_____

_____

What were the dark and twisty parts of today's YESes?

_____

_____

_____

_____

_____

_____

_____

_____

Body

What motivates me to live a healthy life?

_____
_____
_____
_____
_____
_____
_____
_____
_____
_____
_____
_____
_____
_____
_____
_____
_____
_____
_____
_____
_____
_____
_____
_____
_____
_____
_____

Body

DAY 21

The YESes I handled today:

_____

_____

_____

_____

_____

_____

_____

What I gained by saying YES:

_____

_____

_____

_____

_____

_____

_____

What were the dark and twisty parts of today's YESes?

_____

_____

_____

_____

_____

_____

_____

Body

DAY 22

The YESes I handled today:

_____
_____
_____
_____
_____
_____
_____

What I gained by saying YES:

_____
_____
_____
_____
_____
_____
_____

What were the dark and twisty parts of today's YESes?

_____
_____
_____
_____
_____
_____
_____

Body

DAY 23

The YESes I handled today:

_____
_____
_____
_____
_____
_____
_____

What I gained by saying YES:

_____
_____
_____
_____
_____
_____
_____

What were the dark and twisty parts of today's YESes?

_____
_____
_____
_____
_____
_____
_____

Body

DAY 24

The YESes I handled today:

_____
_____
_____
_____
_____
_____
_____

What I gained by saying YES:

_____
_____
_____
_____
_____
_____
_____

What were the dark and twisty parts of today's YESes?

_____
_____
_____
_____
_____
_____
_____

Body

DAY 25

The YESes I handled today:

_____

_____

_____

_____

_____

_____

_____

What I gained by saying YES:

_____

_____

_____

_____

_____

_____

_____

What were the dark and twisty parts of today's YESes?

_____

_____

_____

_____

_____

_____

_____

Body

DAY 26

The YESes I handled today:

_____

_____

_____

_____

_____

_____

_____

What I gained by saying YES:

_____

_____

_____

_____

_____

_____

_____

What were the dark and twisty parts of today's YESes?

_____

_____

_____

_____

_____

_____

_____

Body

DAY 27

The YESes I handled today:

_____

_____

_____

_____

_____

_____

_____

What I gained by saying YES:

_____

_____

_____

_____

_____

_____

_____

What were the dark and twisty parts of today's YESes?

_____

_____

_____

_____

_____

_____

_____

Body

DAY 28

The YESes I handled today:

_____
_____
_____
_____
_____
_____
_____

What I gained by saying YES:

_____
_____
_____
_____
_____
_____
_____

What were the dark and twisty parts of today's YESes?

_____
_____
_____
_____
_____
_____
_____

Body

DAY 29

The YESes I handled today:

_____

_____

_____

_____

_____

_____

What I gained by saying YES:

_____

_____

_____

_____

_____

_____

What were the dark and twisty parts of today's YESes?

_____

_____

_____

_____

_____

_____

_____

Body

DAY 30

The YESes I handled today:

_____
_____
_____
_____
_____
_____
_____

What I gained by saying YES:

_____
_____
_____
_____
_____
_____

What were the dark and twisty parts of today's YESes?

_____
_____
_____
_____
_____
_____
_____

Body

DAY 31

The YESes I handled today:

_____

_____

_____

_____

_____

_____

_____

What I gained by saying YES:

_____

_____

_____

_____

_____

_____

_____

What were the dark and twisty parts of today's YESes?

_____

_____

_____

_____

_____

_____

_____

MONTH FIVE

YES TO PEOPLE

Your people are only worth having around if they
are the RIGHT people. Have no time for untrue friends—
stick with the people who understand YOUR
definition of love and support.

Things I will say YES to this month:

_____
_____
_____
_____
_____
_____
_____
_____
_____
_____
_____

People

Who are my ride or die friends and why?

_____
_____
_____
_____
_____
_____
_____
_____
_____
_____
_____
_____
_____
_____
_____
_____
_____
_____
_____
_____
_____
_____
_____
_____
_____
_____
_____

YES
to
REAL
PEOPLE.

YES
to
TRUE
FRIENDS.

People

DAY 1

The YESes I handled today:

_____

_____

_____

_____

_____

_____

_____

What I gained by saying YES:

_____

_____

_____

_____

_____

_____

_____

What were the dark and twisty parts of today's YESes?

_____

_____

_____

_____

_____

_____

People

DAY 2

The YESes I handled today:

_____
_____
_____
_____
_____
_____
_____

What I gained by saying YES:

_____
_____
_____
_____
_____
_____
_____

What were the dark and twisty parts of today's YESes?

_____
_____
_____
_____
_____
_____
_____

People

DAY 3

The YESes I handled today:

_____
_____
_____
_____
_____
_____
_____
_____

What I gained by saying YES:

_____
_____
_____
_____
_____
_____

What were the dark and twisty parts of today's YESes?

_____
_____
_____
_____
_____
_____
_____

People

DAY 4

The YESes I handled today:

_____

_____

_____

_____

_____

_____

_____

What I gained by saying YES:

_____

_____

_____

_____

_____

_____

_____

What were the dark and twisty parts of today's YESes?

_____

_____

_____

_____

_____

_____

_____

People

DAY 5

The YESes I handled today:

_____
_____
_____
_____
_____
_____
_____

What I gained by saying YES:

_____
_____
_____
_____
_____
_____

What were the dark and twisty parts of today's YESes?

_____
_____
_____
_____
_____
_____

YOUR TRIBE

is

OUT THERE WAITING

for YOU.

GO FIND THEM.

DAY 6

The YESes I handled today:

_____

_____

_____

_____

_____

_____

_____

What I gained by saying YES:

_____

_____

_____

_____

_____

_____

_____

What were the dark and twisty parts of today's YESes?

_____

_____

_____

_____

_____

_____

_____

People

DAY 7

The YESes I handled today:

_____
_____
_____
_____
_____
_____
_____

What I gained by saying YES:

_____
_____
_____
_____
_____
_____
_____

What were the dark and twisty parts of today's YESes?

_____
_____
_____
_____
_____
_____
_____

People

DAY 8

The YESes I handled today:

_____

_____

_____

_____

_____

_____

_____

What I gained by saying YES:

_____

_____

_____

_____

_____

_____

_____

What were the dark and twisty parts of today's YESes?

_____

_____

_____

_____

_____

_____

_____

People

DAY 9

The YESes I handled today:

_____

_____

_____

_____

_____

_____

What I gained by saying YES:

_____

_____

_____

_____

_____

_____

What were the dark and twisty parts of today's YESes?

_____

_____

_____

_____

_____

_____

People

DAY 10

The YESes I handled today:

_____

_____

_____

_____

_____

_____

_____

What I gained by saying YES:

_____

_____

_____

_____

_____

_____

What were the dark and twisty parts of today's YESes?

_____

_____

_____

_____

_____

_____

People

DAY 11

The YESes I handled today:

_____

_____

_____

_____

_____

_____

_____

What I gained by saying YES:

_____

_____

_____

_____

_____

_____

What were the dark and twisty parts of today's YESes?

_____

_____

_____

_____

_____

_____

_____

People

DAY 12

The YESes I handled today:

_____
_____
_____
_____
_____
_____
_____

What I gained by saying YES:

_____
_____
_____
_____
_____
_____
_____

What were the dark and twisty parts of today's YESes?

_____
_____
_____
_____
_____
_____
_____

DAY 13

The YESes I handled today:

_____

_____

_____

_____

_____

_____

What I gained by saying YES:

_____

_____

_____

_____

_____

_____

What were the dark and twisty parts of today's YESes?

_____

_____

_____

_____

_____

_____

_____

People

DAY 14

The YESes I handled today:

_____

_____

_____

_____

_____

_____

What I gained by saying YES:

_____

_____

_____

_____

_____

_____

What were the dark and twisty parts of today's YESes?

_____

_____

_____

_____

_____

_____

People

What are some qualities my friends admire in me?

_____

_____

_____

_____

_____

_____

_____

_____

_____

_____

_____

_____

_____

_____

_____

_____

_____

_____

_____

_____

_____

_____

_____

_____

People

DAY 15

The YESes I handled today:

_____

_____

_____

_____

_____

_____

_____

What I gained by saying YES:

_____

_____

_____

_____

_____

_____

_____

What were the dark and twisty parts of today's YESes?

_____

_____

_____

_____

_____

_____

_____

DAY 16

The YESes I handled today:

_____

_____

_____

_____

_____

_____

_____

What I gained by saying YES:

_____

_____

_____

_____

_____

_____

_____

What were the dark and twisty parts of today's YESes?

_____

_____

_____

_____

_____

_____

_____

People

DAY 17

The YESes I handled today:

_____
_____
_____
_____
_____
_____
_____

What I gained by saying YES:

_____
_____
_____
_____
_____
_____
_____

What were the dark and twisty parts of today's YESes?

_____
_____
_____
_____
_____
_____
_____

People

DAY 18

The YESes I handled today:

_____
_____
_____
_____
_____
_____
_____

What I gained by saying YES:

_____
_____
_____
_____
_____
_____
_____

What were the dark and twisty parts of today's YESes?

_____
_____
_____
_____
_____
_____
_____

People

DAY 19

The YESes I handled today:

_____

_____

_____

_____

_____

_____

What I gained by saying YES:

_____

_____

_____

_____

_____

_____

What were the dark and twisty parts of today's YESes?

_____

_____

_____

_____

_____

_____

DAY 20

The YESes I handled today:

_____

_____

_____

_____

_____

_____

_____

What I gained by saying YES:

_____

_____

_____

_____

_____

_____

_____

What were the dark and twisty parts of today's YESes?

_____

_____

_____

_____

_____

_____

_____

People

DAY 21

The YESes I handled today:

_____
_____
_____
_____
_____
_____
_____

What I gained by saying YES:

_____
_____
_____
_____
_____
_____
_____

What were the dark and twisty parts of today's YESes?

_____
_____
_____
_____
_____
_____
_____

People

DAY 22

The YESes I handled today:

_____

_____

_____

_____

_____

_____

_____

What I gained by saying YES:

_____

_____

_____

_____

_____

_____

_____

What were the dark and twisty parts of today's YESes?

_____

_____

_____

_____

_____

_____

_____

People

DAY 23

The YESes I handled today:

_____
_____
_____
_____
_____
_____
_____

What I gained by saying YES:

_____
_____
_____
_____
_____
_____
_____

What were the dark and twisty parts of today's YESes?

_____
_____
_____
_____
_____
_____
_____

People

DAY 24

The YESes I handled today:

_____
_____
_____
_____
_____
_____
_____

What I gained by saying YES:

_____
_____
_____
_____
_____
_____
_____

What were the dark and twisty parts of today's YESes?

_____
_____
_____
_____
_____
_____
_____

People

DAY 25

The YESes I handled today:

_____
_____
_____
_____
_____
_____
_____

What I gained by saying YES:

_____
_____
_____
_____
_____
_____

What were the dark and twisty parts of today's YESes?

_____
_____
_____
_____
_____
_____
_____

People

DAY 26

The YESes I handled today:

_____

_____

_____

_____

_____

_____

_____

What I gained by saying YES:

_____

_____

_____

_____

_____

_____

_____

What were the dark and twisty parts of today's YESes?

_____

_____

_____

_____

_____

_____

_____

People

DAY 27

The YESes I handled today:

_____
_____
_____
_____
_____
_____
_____

What I gained by saying YES:

_____
_____
_____
_____
_____
_____
_____

What were the dark and twisty parts of today's YESes?

_____
_____
_____
_____
_____
_____
_____

People

DAY 28

The YESes I handled today:

_____
_____
_____
_____
_____
_____
_____

What I gained by saying YES:

_____
_____
_____
_____
_____
_____
_____

What were the dark and twisty parts of today's YESes?

_____
_____
_____
_____
_____
_____
_____

People

DAY 29

The YESes I handled today:

_____
_____
_____
_____
_____
_____
_____

What I gained by saying YES:

_____
_____
_____
_____
_____
_____
_____

What were the dark and twisty parts of today's YESes?

_____
_____
_____
_____
_____
_____
_____

People

DAY 30

The YESes I handled today:

_____
_____
_____
_____
_____
_____
_____

What I gained by saying YES:

_____
_____
_____
_____
_____
_____
_____

What were the dark and twisty parts of today's YESes?

_____
_____
_____
_____
_____
_____
_____

DAY 31

The YESes I handled today:

_____

_____

_____

_____

_____

_____

_____

What I gained by saying YES:

_____

_____

_____

_____

_____

_____

_____

What were the dark and twisty parts of today's YESes?

_____

_____

_____

_____

_____

_____

_____

Help

MONTH SIX

YES TO HELP

Saying "I need help" can feel like failure. Or it can feel like maturity—you have learned how to handle your life and how to take care of your business and your needs.

Things I will say YES to this month:

_____
_____
_____
_____
_____
_____
_____
_____
_____
_____
_____
_____
_____

Help

Most people find it difficult to ask for help. Create a list of people you would consider your support:

_____

_____

_____

_____

_____

_____

_____

_____

_____

_____

_____

_____

_____

_____

_____

_____

_____

_____

_____

_____

_____

_____

_____

_____

_____

_____

"HOW DO

YOU

DO IT ALL?"

The answer is this:

I DON'T.

Help

DAY 1

The YESes I handled today:

_____
_____
_____
_____
_____
_____
_____

What I gained by saying YES:

_____
_____
_____
_____
_____
_____
_____

What were the dark and twisty parts of today's YESes?

_____
_____
_____
_____
_____
_____
_____

Help

DAY 2

The YESes I handled today:

_____

_____

_____

_____

_____

_____

_____

What I gained by saying YES:

_____

_____

_____

_____

_____

_____

_____

What were the dark and twisty parts of today's YESes?

_____

_____

_____

_____

_____

_____

_____

Help

DAY 3

The YESes I handled today:

_____
_____
_____
_____
_____
_____
_____

What I gained by saying YES:

_____
_____
_____
_____
_____
_____
_____

What were the dark and twisty parts of today's YESes?

_____
_____
_____
_____
_____
_____
_____

DAY 4

The YESes I handled today:

_____
_____
_____
_____
_____
_____
_____

What I gained by saying YES:

_____
_____
_____
_____
_____
_____

What were the dark and twisty parts of today's YESes?

_____
_____
_____
_____
_____
_____
_____

Help

DAY 5

The YESes I handled today:

_____
_____
_____
_____
_____
_____
_____

What I gained by saying YES:

_____
_____
_____
_____
_____
_____
_____

What were the dark and twisty parts of today's YESes?

_____
_____
_____
_____
_____
_____
_____

Help

DAY 6

The YESes I handled today:

_____
_____
_____
_____
_____
_____
_____

What I gained by saying YES:

_____
_____
_____
_____
_____
_____
_____

What were the dark and twisty parts of today's YESes?

_____
_____
_____
_____
_____
_____
_____

Help

DAY 7

The YESes I handled today:

_____

_____

_____

_____

_____

_____

_____

What I gained by saying YES:

_____

_____

_____

_____

_____

_____

_____

What were the dark and twisty parts of today's YESes?

_____

_____

_____

_____

_____

_____

_____

Help

DAY 8

The YESes I handled today:

_____

_____

_____

_____

_____

_____

What I gained by saying YES:

_____

_____

_____

_____

_____

_____

What were the dark and twisty parts of today's YESes?

_____

_____

_____

_____

_____

_____

Help

DAY 9

The YESes I handled today:

_____

_____

_____

_____

_____

_____

What I gained by saying YES:

_____

_____

_____

_____

_____

_____

What were the dark and twisty parts of today's YESes?

_____

_____

_____

_____

_____

_____

_____

Help

DAY 10

The YESes I handled today:

_____

_____

_____

_____

_____

_____

_____

What I gained by saying YES:

_____

_____

_____

_____

_____

_____

_____

What were the dark and twisty parts of today's YESes?

_____

_____

_____

_____

_____

_____

_____

Help

DAY 11

The YESes I handled today:

_____
_____
_____
_____
_____
_____
_____

What I gained by saying YES:

_____
_____
_____
_____
_____
_____

What were the dark and twisty parts of today's YESes?

_____
_____
_____
_____
_____
_____

Help

DAY 12

The YESes I handled today:

_____

_____

_____

_____

_____

_____

_____

What I gained by saying YES:

_____

_____

_____

_____

_____

_____

_____

What were the dark and twisty parts of today's YESes?

_____

_____

_____

_____

_____

_____

_____

Help

DAY 13

The YESes I handled today:

_____
_____
_____
_____
_____
_____
_____

What I gained by saying YES:

_____
_____
_____
_____
_____
_____
_____

What were the dark and twisty parts of today's YESes?

_____
_____
_____
_____
_____
_____
_____

Help

DAY 14

The YESes I handled today:

_____

_____

_____

_____

_____

_____

_____

What I gained by saying YES:

_____

_____

_____

_____

_____

_____

_____

What were the dark and twisty parts of today's YESes?

_____

_____

_____

_____

_____

_____

_____

Help

DAY 15

The YESes I handled today:

_____

_____

_____

_____

_____

_____

_____

What I gained by saying YES:

_____

_____

_____

_____

_____

_____

_____

What were the dark and twisty parts of today's YESes?

_____

_____

_____

_____

_____

_____

_____

ANYONE

who

TELLS YOU

they are doing it

✦ ALL ✦

PERFECTLY

is a

LIAR.

Help

DAY 16

The YESes I handled today:

_____

_____

_____

_____

_____

_____

_____

What I gained by saying YES:

_____

_____

_____

_____

_____

_____

_____

What were the dark and twisty parts of today's YESes?

_____

_____

_____

_____

_____

_____

_____

DAY 17

The YESes I handled today:

_____

_____

_____

_____

_____

_____

_____

What I gained by saying YES:

_____

_____

_____

_____

_____

_____

_____

What were the dark and twisty parts of today's YESes?

_____

_____

_____

_____

_____

_____

_____

_____

DAY 18

The YESes I handled today:

_____
_____
_____
_____
_____
_____
_____
_____

What I gained by saying YES:

_____
_____
_____
_____
_____
_____
_____
_____

What were the dark and twisty parts of today's YESes?

_____
_____
_____
_____
_____
_____
_____
_____

Help

DAY 19

The YESes I handled today:

_____

_____

_____

_____

_____

_____

_____

What I gained by saying YES:

_____

_____

_____

_____

_____

_____

_____

What were the dark and twisty parts of today's YESes?

_____

_____

_____

_____

_____

_____

_____

Help

DAY 20

The YESes I handled today:

_____
_____
_____
_____
_____
_____
_____

What I gained by saying YES:

_____
_____
_____
_____
_____
_____

What were the dark and twisty parts of today's YESes?

_____
_____
_____
_____
_____
_____
_____

DAY 21

The YESes I handled today:

_____

_____

_____

_____

_____

_____

_____

What I gained by saying YES:

_____

_____

_____

_____

_____

_____

_____

What were the dark and twisty parts of today's YESes?

_____

_____

_____

_____

_____

_____

_____

DAY 22

The YESes I handled today:

_____

_____

_____

_____

_____

_____

_____

What I gained by saying YES:

_____

_____

_____

_____

_____

_____

_____

What were the dark and twisty parts of today's YESes?

_____

_____

_____

_____

_____

_____

_____

DAY 23

The YESes I handled today:

_____
_____
_____
_____
_____
_____
_____

What I gained by saying YES:

_____
_____
_____
_____
_____
_____

What were the dark and twisty parts of today's YESes?

_____
_____
_____
_____
_____
_____
_____

Help

DAY 24

The YESes I handled today:

_____

_____

_____

_____

_____

_____

_____

What I gained by saying YES:

_____

_____

_____

_____

_____

_____

_____

What were the dark and twisty parts of today's YESes?

_____

_____

_____

_____

_____

_____

_____

DAY 25

The YESes I handled today:

_____

_____

_____

_____

_____

_____

_____

What I gained by saying YES:

_____

_____

_____

_____

_____

_____

_____

What were the dark and twisty parts of today's YESes?

_____

_____

_____

_____

_____

_____

_____

Help

DAY 26

The YESes I handled today:

_____
_____
_____
_____
_____
_____
_____

What I gained by saying YES:

_____
_____
_____
_____
_____
_____
_____

What were the dark and twisty parts of today's YESes?

_____
_____
_____
_____
_____
_____
_____

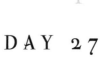

Help

DAY 27

The YESes I handled today:

_____

_____

_____

_____

_____

_____

_____

What I gained by saying YES:

_____

_____

_____

_____

_____

_____

_____

What were the dark and twisty parts of today's YESes?

_____

_____

_____

_____

_____

_____

_____

_____

Help

DAY 28

The YESes I handled today:

_____
_____
_____
_____
_____
_____
_____

What I gained by saying YES:

_____
_____
_____
_____
_____
_____
_____

What were the dark and twisty parts of today's YESes?

_____
_____
_____
_____
_____
_____
_____

DAY 29

The YESes I handled today:

_____

_____

_____

_____

_____

_____

_____

What I gained by saying YES:

_____

_____

_____

_____

_____

_____

_____

What were the dark and twisty parts of today's YESes?

_____

_____

_____

_____

_____

_____

_____

Help

DAY 30

The YESes I handled today:

_____
_____
_____
_____
_____
_____
_____

What I gained by saying YES:

_____
_____
_____
_____
_____
_____
_____

What were the dark and twisty parts of today's YESes?

_____
_____
_____
_____
_____
_____
_____

Help

DAY 31

The YESes I handled today:

_____

_____

_____

_____

_____

_____

_____

What I gained by saying YES:

_____

_____

_____

_____

_____

_____

_____

What were the dark and twisty parts of today's YESes?

_____

_____

_____

_____

_____

_____

_____

SIX-MONTH

CHECK-IN

Why hello! It's been six whole months!

You look good!

Actually, I don't know how you look. But I think you probably look good because I pretty much believe that everyone who isn't an evil, mean, emotional vampire is beautiful. So you look beautiful.

How is your Year of Yes going? Maybe you are feeling empowered and amazing, charging into the world, yessing left and yessing right, all fierce and badass. Or maybe you are like me at my six-month mark, feeling fragile and scared and sad. Maybe you've shed friends. Or you've shed a fiancé. Or you've ended a job. Or a goal you set didn't materialize. Maybe you just feel . . . lost.

Here's the thing: no one said evolution was a party.

I mean, have you seen those photos of that hunched-over dude who couldn't make fire? He had to run from big woolly mammoths and he was probably hungry all the time. That wasn't fun. He was evolving. Into us. So . . . count your blessings.

Seriously, it's not always going to be fun. Or easy. I cried. A lot. Like a giant weepy baby. My sisters did a lot of hollering. "STOP CRYING AND GET UP!" Which helped. Maybe ask someone to remind you to stop crying. Maybe ask a friend to drag you out of the house. Maybe just go be by yourself for at least an hour a week. And if you have small children and can't do that? Lock yourself in the bathroom for ten minutes a day and sing really loud. That helps. At least it helps me.

Have you just . . . stopped? Completely? Are you not yessing at all? Have you given up? Guess what?

STOP GIVING UP!

SAY YES TO SOMETHING RIGHT NOW AND THEN DO IT!!

That's how easy it is to get started again. Whatever happened in the past has no hold on you. It's not like there's some tally being kept. No one is keeping score. Just start over and move on. Yesterday already happened. You can pretend like you don't even know yesterday. You can pass yesterday on the street and act like you did not just see yesterday the other day. You can be all about your new friend tomorrow.

Pick a new *YES* Goal. And do it.

The difference between people whose lives change and those whose lives don't?

The ones whose lives change are the ones who CHANGE THEIR LIVES. The ones who don't? They eat all the fried chicken. And they say no a lot.

You can do it.

Dance it out. Get it together.

And if you have been doing it? You deserve a little celebration.

You may find that it is hard to find someone to celebrate with you. You may find it is hard to find people who are happy for you. Like I said, evolution is no party. Evolution can be lonely. That doesn't mean you don't deserve to celebrate. Even if you are just a party of one.

Party on!

Reflect on the YESes you've accomplished so far this year. What are you most proud of?

_____

_____

_____

_____

_____

_____

_____

_____

_____

_____

_____

_____

_____

_____

_____

_____

_____

_____

_____

_____

_____

_____

_____

_____

_____

_____

Look back at your initial Year of Yes vision. What have you learned?

_____

_____

_____

_____

_____

_____

_____

_____

_____

_____

Do you feel you've changed as a person in these six months? How?

_____

_____

_____

_____

_____

_____

_____

_____

_____

_____

MONTH SEVEN

YES TO SWAGGER

In order to achieve any measure of greatness,
you have to first believe you can be great. Be your own
hype man. Swagger shamelessly. Put a little badassery
into your pursuit of happiness.

Things I will say YES to this month:

_____

_____

_____

_____

_____

_____

_____

_____

_____

_____

_____

_____

_____

Swagger

What are some things that have been holding you back from saying YES?

_____

_____

_____

_____

_____

_____

_____

_____

_____

_____

_____

_____

_____

_____

_____

_____

_____

_____

_____

_____

_____

_____

_____

_____

_____

_____

_____

SPEAK.

Be

HEARD.

Swagger

DAY 1

The YESes I handled today:

_____

_____

_____

_____

_____

_____

_____

What I gained by saying YES:

_____

_____

_____

_____

_____

_____

_____

What were the dark and twisty parts of today's YESes?

_____

_____

_____

_____

_____

_____

_____

Swagger

DAY 2

The YESes I handled today:

_____

_____

_____

_____

_____

_____

_____

What I gained by saying YES:

_____

_____

_____

_____

_____

_____

_____

What were the dark and twisty parts of today's YESes?

_____

_____

_____

_____

_____

_____

_____

Swagger

DAY 3

The YESes I handled today:

_____

_____

_____

_____

_____

_____

_____

What I gained by saying YES:

_____

_____

_____

_____

_____

_____

_____

What were the dark and twisty parts of today's YESes?

_____

_____

_____

_____

_____

_____

Swagger

DAY 4

The YESes I handled today:

_____
_____
_____
_____
_____
_____
_____

What I gained by saying YES:

_____
_____
_____
_____
_____
_____
_____

What were the dark and twisty parts of today's YESes?

_____
_____
_____
_____
_____
_____
_____

Swagger

DAY 5

The YESes I handled today:

_____

_____

_____

_____

_____

_____

What I gained by saying YES:

_____

_____

_____

_____

_____

_____

What were the dark and twisty parts of today's YESes?

_____

_____

_____

_____

_____

_____

Swagger

DAY 6

The YESes I handled today:

_____
_____
_____
_____
_____
_____
_____

What I gained by saying YES:

_____
_____
_____
_____
_____
_____
_____

What were the dark and twisty parts of today's YESes?

_____
_____
_____
_____
_____
_____
_____

Swagger

DAY 7

The YESes I handled today:

_____
_____
_____
_____
_____
_____
_____

What I gained by saying YES:

_____
_____
_____
_____
_____
_____
_____

What were the dark and twisty parts of today's YESes?

_____
_____
_____
_____
_____
_____
_____

Swagger

DAY 8

The YESes I handled today:

_____

_____

_____

_____

_____

_____

_____

What I gained by saying YES:

_____

_____

_____

_____

_____

_____

_____

What were the dark and twisty parts of today's YESes?

_____

_____

_____

_____

_____

_____

_____

Swagger

DAY 9

The YESes I handled today:

_____
_____
_____
_____
_____
_____
_____

What I gained by saying YES:

_____
_____
_____
_____
_____
_____
_____

What were the dark and twisty parts of today's YESes?

_____
_____
_____
_____
_____
_____
_____
_____

Swagger

DAY 10

The YESes I handled today:

_____
_____
_____
_____
_____
_____
_____

What I gained by saying YES:

_____
_____
_____
_____
_____
_____
_____

What were the dark and twisty parts of today's YESes?

_____
_____
_____
_____
_____
_____
_____

Swagger

DAY 11

The YESes I handled today:

_____

_____

_____

_____

_____

_____

_____

What I gained by saying YES:

_____

_____

_____

_____

_____

_____

What were the dark and twisty parts of today's YESes?

_____

_____

_____

_____

_____

_____

_____

Swagger

DAY 12

The YESes I handled today:

_____

_____

_____

_____

_____

_____

_____

What I gained by saying YES:

_____

_____

_____

_____

_____

_____

_____

What were the dark and twisty parts of today's YESes?

_____

_____

_____

_____

_____

_____

_____

Swagger

DAY 13

The YESes I handled today:

_____
_____
_____
_____
_____
_____
_____

What I gained by saying YES:

_____
_____
_____
_____
_____
_____

What were the dark and twisty parts of today's YESes?

_____
_____
_____
_____
_____
_____

Swagger

DAY 14

The YESes I handled today:

_____
_____
_____
_____
_____
_____
_____

What I gained by saying YES:

_____
_____
_____
_____
_____
_____
_____

What were the dark and twisty parts of today's YESes?

_____
_____
_____
_____
_____
_____
_____

Swagger

DAY 15

The YESes I handled today:

_____
_____
_____
_____
_____
_____
_____

What I gained by saying YES:

_____
_____
_____
_____
_____
_____

What were the dark and twisty parts of today's YESes?

_____
_____
_____
_____
_____
_____
_____

EVERY SINGLE TIME

you get the chance,

STAND UP

in front of people.

LET THEM SEE YOU.

Swagger

DAY 16

The YESes I handled today:

_____
_____
_____
_____
_____
_____
_____

What I gained by saying YES:

_____
_____
_____
_____
_____
_____
_____

What were the dark and twisty parts of today's YESes?

_____
_____
_____
_____
_____
_____
_____

DAY 17

The YESes I handled today:

_____
_____
_____
_____
_____
_____
_____

What I gained by saying YES:

_____
_____
_____
_____
_____
_____
_____

What were the dark and twisty parts of today's YESes?

_____
_____
_____
_____
_____
_____
_____

Swagger

DAY 18

The YESes I handled today:

_____

_____

_____

_____

_____

_____

_____

What I gained by saying YES:

_____

_____

_____

_____

_____

_____

_____

What were the dark and twisty parts of today's YESes?

_____

_____

_____

_____

_____

_____

_____

Swagger

DAY 19

The YESes I handled today:

_____

_____

_____

_____

_____

_____

What I gained by saying YES:

_____

_____

_____

_____

_____

_____

What were the dark and twisty parts of today's YESes?

_____

_____

_____

_____

_____

_____

_____

DAY 20

The YESes I handled today:

_____

_____

_____

_____

_____

_____

_____

What I gained by saying YES:

_____

_____

_____

_____

_____

_____

What were the dark and twisty parts of today's YESes?

_____

_____

_____

_____

_____

_____

I had
NOT
FAILED.

I just

DIDN'T

OWN

THE WIG.

Swagger

DAY 21

The YESes I handled today:

_____
_____
_____
_____
_____
_____
_____

What I gained by saying YES:

_____
_____
_____
_____
_____
_____
_____

What were the dark and twisty parts of today's YESes?

_____
_____
_____
_____
_____
_____
_____

Swagger

DAY 22

The YESes I handled today:

_____

_____

_____

_____

_____

_____

_____

What I gained by saying YES:

_____

_____

_____

_____

_____

_____

_____

What were the dark and twisty parts of today's YESes?

_____

_____

_____

_____

_____

_____

_____

Swagger

DAY 23

The YESes I handled today:

_____

_____

_____

_____

_____

_____

_____

What I gained by saying YES:

_____

_____

_____

_____

_____

_____

_____

What were the dark and twisty parts of today's YESes?

_____

_____

_____

_____

_____

_____

_____

Swagger

DAY 24

The YESes I handled today:

_____
_____
_____
_____
_____
_____
_____

What I gained by saying YES:

_____
_____
_____
_____
_____
_____
_____

What were the dark and twisty parts of today's YESes?

_____
_____
_____
_____
_____
_____
_____

Swagger

DAY 25

The YESes I handled today:

_____
_____
_____
_____
_____
_____
_____

What I gained by saying YES:

_____
_____
_____
_____
_____
_____

What were the dark and twisty parts of today's YESes?

_____
_____
_____
_____
_____
_____
_____

Swagger

DAY 26

The YESes I handled today:

_____
_____
_____
_____
_____
_____
_____
_____

What I gained by saying YES:

_____
_____
_____
_____
_____
_____
_____

What were the dark and twisty parts of today's YESes?

_____
_____
_____
_____
_____
_____
_____
_____

Swagger

DAY 27

The YESes I handled today:

_____
_____
_____
_____
_____
_____
_____

What I gained by saying YES:

_____
_____
_____
_____
_____
_____
_____

What were the dark and twisty parts of today's YESes?

_____
_____
_____
_____
_____
_____
_____
_____

Swagger

DAY 28

The YESes I handled today:

_____

_____

_____

_____

_____

_____

_____

What I gained by saying YES:

_____

_____

_____

_____

_____

_____

What were the dark and twisty parts of today's YESes?

_____

_____

_____

_____

_____

_____

_____

I can

EXPERIENCE

LIFE

 or I can

GIVE

UP

ON IT.

Swagger

DAY 29

The YESes I handled today:

_____

_____

_____

_____

_____

_____

_____

What I gained by saying YES:

_____

_____

_____

_____

_____

_____

_____

What were the dark and twisty parts of today's YESes?

_____

_____

_____

_____

_____

_____

_____

DAY 30

The YESes I handled today:

_____

_____

_____

_____

_____

_____

What I gained by saying YES:

_____

_____

_____

_____

_____

_____

What were the dark and twisty parts of today's YESes?

_____

_____

_____

_____

_____

_____

Swagger

DAY 31

The YESes I handled today:

_____
_____
_____
_____
_____
_____
_____
_____

What I gained by saying YES:

_____
_____
_____
_____
_____
_____
_____
_____

What were the dark and twisty parts of today's YESes?

_____
_____
_____
_____
_____
_____
_____
_____

MONTH EIGHT

YES TO COMPLIMENTS

Like yourself. Love yourself. Be into yourself.
Think highly of YOU. And say, "Thank you."

Things I will say YES to this month:

_____

_____

_____

_____

_____

_____

_____

_____

_____

_____

_____

_____

_____

_____

_____

Compliments

What are the qualities I love about myself?

Be

BRAVE.

Be

AMAZING.

Be

WORTHY.

Compliments

DAY 1

The YESes I handled today:

_____

_____

_____

_____

_____

_____

_____

What I gained by saying YES:

_____

_____

_____

_____

_____

_____

_____

What were the dark and twisty parts of today's YESes?

_____

_____

_____

_____

_____

_____

_____

Compliments

DAY 2

The YESes I handled today:

_____
_____
_____
_____
_____
_____
_____

What I gained by saying YES:

_____
_____
_____
_____
_____
_____
_____

What were the dark and twisty parts of today's YESes?

_____
_____
_____
_____
_____
_____
_____

Compliments

DAY 3

The YESes I handled today:

_____
_____
_____
_____
_____
_____
_____

What I gained by saying YES:

_____
_____
_____
_____
_____
_____
_____

What were the dark and twisty parts of today's YESes?

_____
_____
_____
_____
_____
_____
_____

Compliments

DAY 4

The YESes I handled today:

_____
_____
_____
_____
_____
_____
_____

What I gained by saying YES:

_____
_____
_____
_____
_____
_____
_____

What were the dark and twisty parts of today's YESes?

_____
_____
_____
_____
_____
_____
_____
_____

Compliments

DAY 5

The YESes I handled today:

_____
_____
_____
_____
_____
_____
_____

What I gained by saying YES:

_____
_____
_____
_____
_____
_____
_____

What were the dark and twisty parts of today's YESes?

_____
_____
_____
_____
_____
_____
_____

Compliments

DAY 6

The YESes I handled today:

_____

_____

_____

_____

_____

_____

_____

What I gained by saying YES:

_____

_____

_____

_____

_____

_____

_____

What were the dark and twisty parts of today's YESes?

_____

_____

_____

_____

_____

_____

_____

Compliments

DAY 7

The YESes I handled today:

_____
_____
_____
_____
_____
_____
_____

What I gained by saying YES:

_____
_____
_____
_____
_____
_____
_____

What were the dark and twisty parts of today's YESes?

_____
_____
_____
_____
_____
_____
_____

Compliments

DAY 8

The YESes I handled today:

_____

_____

_____

_____

_____

_____

_____

What I gained by saying YES:

_____

_____

_____

_____

_____

_____

_____

What were the dark and twisty parts of today's YESes?

_____

_____

_____

_____

_____

_____

_____

Compliments

DAY 9

The YESes I handled today:

_____

_____

_____

_____

_____

_____

_____

What I gained by saying YES:

_____

_____

_____

_____

_____

_____

_____

What were the dark and twisty parts of today's YESes?

_____

_____

_____

_____

_____

_____

_____

Compliments

DAY 10

The YESes I handled today:

_____
_____
_____
_____
_____
_____
_____

What I gained by saying YES:

_____
_____
_____
_____
_____
_____

What were the dark and twisty parts of today's YESes?

_____
_____
_____
_____
_____
_____

THANK
YOU.

SMILE.

SHUT
UP.

Compliments

DAY 11

The YESes I handled today:

_____

_____

_____

_____

_____

_____

_____

What I gained by saying YES:

_____

_____

_____

_____

_____

_____

_____

What were the dark and twisty parts of today's YESes?

_____

_____

_____

_____

_____

_____

_____

Compliments

DAY 12

The YESes I handled today:

_____

_____

_____

_____

_____

_____

_____

What I gained by saying YES:

_____

_____

_____

_____

_____

_____

What were the dark and twisty parts of today's YESes?

_____

_____

_____

_____

_____

_____

Compliments

DAY 13

The YESes I handled today:

_____

_____

_____

_____

_____

_____

_____

What I gained by saying YES:

_____

_____

_____

_____

_____

_____

_____

What were the dark and twisty parts of today's YESes?

_____

_____

_____

_____

_____

_____

_____

DAY 14

The YESes I handled today:

_____
_____
_____
_____
_____
_____
_____

What I gained by saying YES:

_____
_____
_____
_____
_____
_____
_____

What were the dark and twisty parts of today's YESes?

_____
_____
_____
_____
_____
_____
_____

Compliments

DAY 15

The YESes I handled today:

_____

_____

_____

_____

_____

_____

_____

What I gained by saying YES:

_____

_____

_____

_____

_____

_____

_____

What were the dark and twisty parts of today's YESes?

_____

_____

_____

_____

_____

_____

_____

Compliments

DAY 16

The YESes I handled today:

_____

_____

_____

_____

_____

_____

_____

What I gained by saying YES:

_____

_____

_____

_____

_____

_____

_____

What were the dark and twisty parts of today's YESes?

_____

_____

_____

_____

_____

_____

_____

Compliments

DAY 17

The YESes I handled today:

_____
_____
_____
_____
_____
_____
_____

What I gained by saying YES:

_____
_____
_____
_____
_____
_____
_____

What were the dark and twisty parts of today's YESes?

_____
_____
_____
_____
_____
_____
_____

Compliments

DAY 18

The YESes I handled today:

_____

_____

_____

_____

_____

_____

_____

What I gained by saying YES:

_____

_____

_____

_____

_____

_____

_____

What were the dark and twisty parts of today's YESes?

_____

_____

_____

_____

_____

_____

_____

Compliments

DAY 19

The YESes I handled today:

_____

_____

_____

_____

_____

_____

_____

What I gained by saying YES:

_____

_____

_____

_____

_____

_____

_____

What were the dark and twisty parts of today's YESes?

_____

_____

_____

_____

_____

_____

_____

_____

Compliments

DAY 20

The YESes I handled today:

_____
_____
_____
_____
_____
_____
_____

What I gained by saying YES:

_____
_____
_____
_____
_____
_____
_____

What were the dark and twisty parts of today's YESes?

_____
_____
_____
_____
_____
_____
_____

Compliments

DAY 21

The YESes I handled today:

_____
_____
_____
_____
_____
_____
_____

What I gained by saying YES:

_____
_____
_____
_____
_____
_____
_____

What were the dark and twisty parts of today's YESes?

_____
_____
_____
_____
_____
_____
_____

I HAVE

to be

MY

OWN

GREETING CARD.

Compliments

DAY 22

The YESes I handled today:

_____

_____

_____

_____

_____

_____

_____

What I gained by saying YES:

_____

_____

_____

_____

_____

_____

_____

What were the dark and twisty parts of today's YESes?

_____

_____

_____

_____

_____

_____

_____

Compliments

DAY 23

The YESes I handled today:

_____
_____
_____
_____
_____
_____
_____

What I gained by saying YES:

_____
_____
_____
_____
_____
_____
_____

What were the dark and twisty parts of today's YESes?

_____
_____
_____
_____
_____
_____
_____

Compliments

DAY 24

The YESes I handled today:

_____
_____
_____
_____
_____
_____
_____

What I gained by saying YES:

_____
_____
_____
_____
_____
_____
_____

What were the dark and twisty parts of today's YESes?

_____
_____
_____
_____
_____
_____
_____

DAY 25

The YESes I handled today:

_____
_____
_____
_____
_____
_____
_____

What I gained by saying YES:

_____
_____
_____
_____
_____
_____
_____

What were the dark and twisty parts of today's YESes?

_____
_____
_____
_____
_____
_____
_____

Compliments

DAY 26

The YESes I handled today:

_____

_____

_____

_____

_____

_____

_____

What I gained by saying YES:

_____

_____

_____

_____

_____

_____

_____

What were the dark and twisty parts of today's YESes?

_____

_____

_____

_____

_____

_____

_____

DAY 27

The YESes I handled today:

_____

_____

_____

_____

_____

_____

_____

What I gained by saying YES:

_____

_____

_____

_____

_____

_____

_____

What were the dark and twisty parts of today's YESes?

_____

_____

_____

_____

_____

_____

_____

Compliments

DAY 28

The YESes I handled today:

_____

_____

_____

_____

_____

_____

_____

What I gained by saying YES:

_____

_____

_____

_____

_____

_____

_____

What were the dark and twisty parts of today's YESes?

_____

_____

_____

_____

_____

_____

_____

Compliments

DAY 29

The YESes I handled today:

_____
_____
_____
_____
_____
_____
_____

What I gained by saying YES:

_____
_____
_____
_____
_____
_____
_____

What were the dark and twisty parts of today's YESes?

_____
_____
_____
_____
_____
_____
_____

Compliments

DAY 30

The YESes I handled today:

_____
_____
_____
_____
_____
_____
_____

What I gained by saying YES:

_____
_____
_____
_____
_____
_____
_____

What were the dark and twisty parts of today's YESes?

_____
_____
_____
_____
_____
_____
_____

DAY 31

The YESes I handled today:

_____
_____
_____
_____
_____
_____
_____

What I gained by saying YES:

_____
_____
_____
_____
_____
_____
_____

What were the dark and twisty parts of today's YESes?

_____
_____
_____
_____
_____
_____
_____

MONTH NINE

YES TO MORE YES

How far can you go? How much can you challenge
yourself? Why limit yourself? Do YOU!

Things I will say YES to this month:

_____

_____

_____

_____

_____

_____

_____

_____

_____

_____

_____

_____

_____

_____

Yes

How is saying YES changing you?

_____

_____

_____

_____

_____

_____

_____

_____

_____

_____

_____

_____

_____

_____

_____

_____

_____

_____

_____

_____

_____

_____

_____

_____

_____

_____

_____

YES

to

EVERYTHING.

EVERYTHING.

Say

YES.

DAY 1

The YESes I handled today:

_____

_____

_____

_____

_____

_____

_____

What I gained by saying YES:

_____

_____

_____

_____

_____

_____

_____

What were the dark and twisty parts of today's YESes?

_____

_____

_____

_____

_____

_____

_____

Yes

DAY 2

The YESes I handled today:

_____

_____

_____

_____

_____

_____

_____

What I gained by saying YES:

_____

_____

_____

_____

_____

_____

_____

What were the dark and twisty parts of today's YESes?

_____

_____

_____

_____

_____

_____

_____

Yes

DAY 3

The YESes I handled today:

_____

_____

_____

_____

_____

_____

_____

What I gained by saying YES:

_____

_____

_____

_____

_____

_____

_____

What were the dark and twisty parts of today's YESes?

_____

_____

_____

_____

_____

_____

_____

Yes

DAY 4

The YESes I handled today:

_____
_____
_____
_____
_____
_____
_____

What I gained by saying YES:

_____
_____
_____
_____
_____
_____
_____

What were the dark and twisty parts of today's YESes?

_____
_____
_____
_____
_____
_____

Yes

DAY 5

The YESes I handled today:

_____
_____
_____
_____
_____
_____
_____

What I gained by saying YES:

_____
_____
_____
_____
_____
_____
_____

What were the dark and twisty parts of today's YESes?

_____
_____
_____
_____
_____
_____
_____

Yes

DAY 6

The YESes I handled today:

_____
_____
_____
_____
_____
_____
_____

What I gained by saying YES:

_____
_____
_____
_____
_____
_____
_____

What were the dark and twisty parts of today's YESes?

_____
_____
_____
_____
_____
_____
_____

Yes

DAY 7

The YESes I handled today:

_____
_____
_____
_____
_____
_____
_____

What I gained by saying YES:

_____
_____
_____
_____
_____
_____
_____

What were the dark and twisty parts of today's YESes?

_____
_____
_____
_____
_____
_____
_____

Yes

DAY 8

The YESes I handled today:

_____

_____

_____

_____

_____

_____

_____

What I gained by saying YES:

_____

_____

_____

_____

_____

_____

_____

What were the dark and twisty parts of today's YESes?

_____

_____

_____

_____

_____

_____

_____

Yes

DAY 9

The YESes I handled today:

_____

_____

_____

_____

_____

_____

_____

What I gained by saying YES:

_____

_____

_____

_____

_____

_____

_____

What were the dark and twisty parts of today's YESes?

_____

_____

_____

_____

_____

_____

_____

Yes

DAY 10

The YESes I handled today:

_____

_____

_____

_____

_____

_____

_____

What I gained by saying YES:

_____

_____

_____

_____

_____

_____

_____

What were the dark and twisty parts of today's YESes?

_____

_____

_____

_____

_____

_____

_____

Yes

DAY 11

The YESes I handled today:

_____

_____

_____

_____

_____

_____

_____

What I gained by saying YES:

_____

_____

_____

_____

_____

_____

_____

What were the dark and twisty parts of today's YESes?

_____

_____

_____

_____

_____

_____

_____

Yes

DAY 12

The YESes I handled today:

_____
_____
_____
_____
_____
_____
_____

What I gained by saying YES:

_____
_____
_____
_____
_____
_____
_____

What were the dark and twisty parts of today's YESes?

_____
_____
_____
_____
_____
_____
_____

Yes

DAY 13

The YESes I handled today:

_____
_____
_____
_____
_____
_____
_____

What I gained by saying YES:

_____
_____
_____
_____
_____
_____
_____

What were the dark and twisty parts of today's YESes?

_____
_____
_____
_____
_____
_____
_____

Yes

DAY 14

The YESes I handled today:

_____
_____
_____
_____
_____
_____
_____

What I gained by saying YES:

_____
_____
_____
_____
_____
_____
_____

What were the dark and twisty parts of today's YESes?

_____
_____
_____
_____
_____
_____
_____

Yes

DAY 15

The YESes I handled today:

_____
_____
_____
_____
_____
_____
_____

What I gained by saying YES:

_____
_____
_____
_____
_____
_____
_____

What were the dark and twisty parts of today's YESes?

_____
_____
_____
_____
_____
_____
_____

Yes

What has been holding me back from saying YES?

_____

_____

_____

_____

_____

_____

_____

_____

_____

_____

_____

_____

_____

_____

_____

_____

_____

_____

_____

_____

_____

_____

_____

_____

_____

_____

_____

_____

_____

_____

_____

_____

Yes

DAY 16

The YESes I handled today:

_____
_____
_____
_____
_____
_____
_____

What I gained by saying YES:

_____
_____
_____
_____
_____
_____
_____

What were the dark and twisty parts of today's YESes?

_____
_____
_____
_____
_____
_____
_____

Yes

DAY 17

The YESes I handled today:

_____
_____
_____
_____
_____
_____
_____

What I gained by saying YES:

_____
_____
_____
_____
_____
_____
_____

What were the dark and twisty parts of today's YESes?

_____
_____
_____
_____
_____
_____
_____

Yes

DAY 18

The YESes I handled today:

_____
_____
_____
_____
_____
_____
_____

What I gained by saying YES:

_____
_____
_____
_____
_____
_____
_____

What were the dark and twisty parts of today's YESes?

_____
_____
_____
_____
_____
_____
_____

Yes

DAY 19

The YESes I handled today:

_____

_____

_____

_____

_____

_____

What I gained by saying YES:

_____

_____

_____

_____

_____

_____

What were the dark and twisty parts of today's YESes?

_____

_____

_____

_____

_____

_____

SAYING YES

is the

SUN.

SAYING YES

is

LIFE.

Yes

DAY 20

The YESes I handled today:

_____

_____

_____

_____

_____

_____

What I gained by saying YES:

_____

_____

_____

_____

_____

_____

What were the dark and twisty parts of today's YESes?

_____

_____

_____

_____

_____

_____

_____

Yes

DAY 21

The YESes I handled today:

_____
_____
_____
_____
_____
_____
_____

What I gained by saying YES:

_____
_____
_____
_____
_____
_____
_____

What were the dark and twisty parts of today's YESes?

_____
_____
_____
_____
_____
_____
_____

Yes

DAY 22

The YESes I handled today:

_____

_____

_____

_____

_____

_____

_____

What I gained by saying YES:

_____

_____

_____

_____

_____

_____

_____

What were the dark and twisty parts of today's YESes?

_____

_____

_____

_____

_____

_____

_____

Yes

DAY 23

The YESes I handled today:

_____

_____

_____

_____

_____

_____

What I gained by saying YES:

_____

_____

_____

_____

_____

_____

What were the dark and twisty parts of today's YESes?

_____

_____

_____

_____

_____

_____

Yes

DAY 24

The YESes I handled today:

_____
_____
_____
_____
_____
_____
_____

What I gained by saying YES:

_____
_____
_____
_____
_____
_____

What were the dark and twisty parts of today's YESes?

_____
_____
_____
_____
_____
_____

Yes

DAY 25

The YESes I handled today:

_____
_____
_____
_____
_____
_____

What I gained by saying YES:

_____
_____
_____
_____
_____
_____

What were the dark and twisty parts of today's YESes?

_____
_____
_____
_____
_____
_____

Yes

DAY 26

The YESes I handled today:

_____
_____
_____
_____
_____
_____
_____

What I gained by saying YES:

_____
_____
_____
_____
_____
_____
_____

What were the dark and twisty parts of today's YESes?

_____
_____
_____
_____
_____
_____
_____

Yes

DAY 27

The YESes I handled today:

_____

_____

_____

_____

_____

_____

_____

What I gained by saying YES:

_____

_____

_____

_____

_____

_____

What were the dark and twisty parts of today's YESes?

_____

_____

_____

_____

_____

_____

Yes

DAY 28

The YESes I handled today:

What I gained by saying YES:

What were the dark and twisty parts of today's YESes?

Yes

DAY 29

The YESes I handled today:

_____

_____

_____

_____

_____

_____

_____

What I gained by saying YES:

_____

_____

_____

_____

_____

_____

_____

What were the dark and twisty parts of today's YESes?

_____

_____

_____

_____

_____

_____

_____

Yes

What are some YESes that have empowered me?

_____

_____

_____

_____

_____

_____

_____

_____

_____

_____

_____

_____

_____

_____

_____

_____

_____

_____

_____

_____

_____

_____

_____

_____

_____

_____

_____

_____

_____

I've just figured

out how to have a

LITTLE

SWAGGER.

———— ◇ ————

I can't stop now.

———— ◇ ————

Yes

DAY 30

The YESes I handled today:

_____

_____

_____

_____

_____

_____

_____

What I gained by saying YES:

_____

_____

_____

_____

_____

_____

_____

What were the dark and twisty parts of today's YESes?

_____

_____

_____

_____

_____

_____

_____

Yes

DAY 31

The YESes I handled today:

_____

_____

_____

_____

_____

_____

_____

What I gained by saying YES:

_____

_____

_____

_____

_____

_____

_____

What were the dark and twisty parts of today's YESes?

_____

_____

_____

_____

_____

_____

_____

MONTH TEN

YES TO DIFFICULT CONVERSATIONS

The things we are afraid to say diminish us by wasting SO much time and energy. Speak. Be honest. Be heard. The conversations you spend so much time avoiding are the ones with the possibility for the most relief.

Things I will say YES to this month:

_____
_____
_____
_____
_____
_____
_____
_____
_____
_____
_____

Conversations

In what situations are you afraid to have difficult conversations?

_____

_____

_____

_____

_____

_____

_____

_____

_____

_____

What are the possible outcomes of your difficult conversations?

_____

_____

_____

_____

_____

_____

_____

_____

_____

_____

_____

FREEDOM

—— • LIES • ——

ACROSS THE

—— • FIELD OF • ——

DIFFICULT

CONVERSATIONS.

DAY 1

The YESes I handled today:

_____
_____
_____
_____
_____
_____
_____

What I gained by saying YES:

_____
_____
_____
_____
_____
_____
_____

What were the dark and twisty parts of today's YESes?

_____
_____
_____
_____
_____
_____
_____

Conversations

DAY 2

The YESes I handled today:

_____
_____
_____
_____
_____
_____
_____

What I gained by saying YES:

_____
_____
_____
_____
_____
_____
_____

What were the dark and twisty parts of today's YESes?

_____
_____
_____
_____
_____
_____
_____

Conversations

DAY 3

The YESes I handled today:

_____

_____

_____

_____

_____

_____

_____

What I gained by saying YES:

_____

_____

_____

_____

_____

_____

_____

What were the dark and twisty parts of today's YESes?

_____

_____

_____

_____

_____

_____

_____

Conversations

DAY 4

The YESes I handled today:

_____
_____
_____
_____
_____
_____
_____

What I gained by saying YES:

_____
_____
_____
_____
_____
_____
_____

What were the dark and twisty parts of today's YESes?

_____
_____
_____
_____
_____
_____

Conversations

DAY 5

The YESes I handled today:

_____

_____

_____

_____

_____

_____

_____

What I gained by saying YES:

_____

_____

_____

_____

_____

_____

_____

What were the dark and twisty parts of today's YESes?

_____

_____

_____

_____

_____

_____

_____

Conversations

DAY 6

The YESes I handled today:

_____

_____

_____

_____

_____

_____

_____

What I gained by saying YES:

_____

_____

_____

_____

_____

_____

What were the dark and twisty parts of today's YESes?

_____

_____

_____

_____

_____

_____

_____

Conversations

DAY 7

The YESes I handled today:

_____
_____
_____
_____
_____
_____
_____

What I gained by saying YES:

_____
_____
_____
_____
_____
_____
_____

What were the dark and twisty parts of today's YESes?

_____
_____
_____
_____
_____
_____
_____

DAY 8

The YESes I handled today:

_____

_____

_____

_____

_____

_____

What I gained by saying YES:

_____

_____

_____

_____

_____

_____

What were the dark and twisty parts of today's YESes?

_____

_____

_____

_____

_____

_____

Conversations

DAY 9

The YESes I handled today:

_____
_____
_____
_____
_____
_____
_____

What I gained by saying YES:

_____
_____
_____
_____
_____
_____
_____

What were the dark and twisty parts of today's YESes?

_____
_____
_____
_____
_____
_____
_____

Conversations

DAY 10

The YESes I handled today:

_____

_____

_____

_____

_____

_____

_____

What I gained by saying YES:

_____

_____

_____

_____

_____

_____

_____

What were the dark and twisty parts of today's YESes?

_____

_____

_____

_____

_____

_____

_____

DAY 11

The YESes I handled today:

_____
_____
_____
_____
_____
_____
_____

What I gained by saying YES:

_____
_____
_____
_____
_____
_____
_____

What were the dark and twisty parts of today's YESes?

_____
_____
_____
_____
_____
_____
_____

Conversations

DAY 12

The YESes I handled today:

_____

_____

_____

_____

_____

_____

_____

What I gained by saying YES:

_____

_____

_____

_____

_____

_____

_____

What were the dark and twisty parts of today's YESes?

_____

_____

_____

_____

_____

_____

_____

Conversations

DAY 13

The YESes I handled today:

_____
_____
_____
_____
_____
_____
_____

What I gained by saying YES:

_____
_____
_____
_____
_____
_____
_____

What were the dark and twisty parts of today's YESes?

_____
_____
_____
_____
_____
_____
_____

Conversations

DAY 14

The YESes I handled today:

_____
_____
_____
_____
_____
_____
_____

What I gained by saying YES:

_____
_____
_____
_____
_____
_____

What were the dark and twisty parts of today's YESes?

_____
_____
_____
_____
_____
_____
_____

Conversations

What phrases will help me stand my ground in difficult conversations?

_____

_____

_____

_____

_____

_____

_____

_____

_____

_____

_____

_____

_____

_____

_____

_____

_____

_____

_____

_____

_____

_____

_____

_____

_____

_____

_____

NO

is

POWERFUL.

It's a big

WEAPON

to

HAVE

in your arsenal. But it

is a very tough

WEAPON to DEPLOY.

Conversations

DAY 15

The YESes I handled today:

_____

_____

_____

_____

_____

_____

_____

What I gained by saying YES:

_____

_____

_____

_____

_____

_____

_____

What were the dark and twisty parts of today's YESes?

_____

_____

_____

_____

_____

_____

_____

Conversations

DAY 16

The YESes I handled today:

_____
_____
_____
_____
_____
_____
_____

What I gained by saying YES:

_____
_____
_____
_____
_____
_____

What were the dark and twisty parts of today's YESes?

_____
_____
_____
_____
_____
_____

Conversations

DAY 17

The YESes I handled today:

_____

_____

_____

_____

_____

_____

_____

What I gained by saying YES:

_____

_____

_____

_____

_____

_____

_____

What were the dark and twisty parts of today's YESes?

_____

_____

_____

_____

_____

_____

_____

DAY 18

The YESes I handled today:

_____

_____

_____

_____

_____

_____

_____

What I gained by saying YES:

_____

_____

_____

_____

_____

_____

_____

What were the dark and twisty parts of today's YESes?

_____

_____

_____

_____

_____

_____

_____

Conversations

DAY 19

The YESes I handled today:

_____

_____

_____

_____

_____

_____

_____

What I gained by saying YES:

_____

_____

_____

_____

_____

_____

_____

What were the dark and twisty parts of today's YESes?

_____

_____

_____

_____

_____

_____

_____

Conversations

DAY 20

The YESes I handled today:

_____
_____
_____
_____
_____
_____

What I gained by saying YES:

_____
_____
_____
_____
_____
_____

What were the dark and twisty parts of today's YESes?

_____
_____
_____
_____
_____
_____

Conversations

DAY 21

The YESes I handled today:

_____

_____

_____

_____

_____

_____

_____

What I gained by saying YES:

_____

_____

_____

_____

_____

_____

_____

What were the dark and twisty parts of today's YESes?

_____

_____

_____

_____

_____

_____

_____

DAY 22

The YESes I handled today:

_____
_____
_____
_____
_____
_____
_____

What I gained by saying YES:

_____
_____
_____
_____
_____
_____
_____

What were the dark and twisty parts of today's YESes?

_____
_____
_____
_____
_____
_____
_____

Conversations

DAY 23

The YESes I handled today:

_____

_____

_____

_____

_____

_____

_____

What I gained by saying YES:

_____

_____

_____

_____

_____

_____

_____

What were the dark and twisty parts of today's YESes?

_____

_____

_____

_____

_____

_____

_____

Conversations

DAY 24

The YESes I handled today:

_____
_____
_____
_____
_____
_____
_____

What I gained by saying YES:

_____
_____
_____
_____
_____
_____
_____

What were the dark and twisty parts of today's YESes?

_____
_____
_____
_____
_____
_____
_____

Conversations

DAY 25

The YESes I handled today:

_____

_____

_____

_____

_____

_____

_____

What I gained by saying YES:

_____

_____

_____

_____

_____

_____

_____

What were the dark and twisty parts of today's YESes?

_____

_____

_____

_____

_____

_____

_____

Conversations

DAY 26

The YESes I handled today:

_____

_____

_____

_____

_____

_____

_____

_____

What I gained by saying YES:

_____

_____

_____

_____

_____

_____

_____

_____

What were the dark and twisty parts of today's YESes?

_____

_____

_____

_____

_____

_____

_____

Conversations

DAY 27

The YESes I handled today:

_____
_____
_____
_____
_____
_____
_____

What I gained by saying YES:

_____
_____
_____
_____
_____
_____
_____

What were the dark and twisty parts of today's YESes?

_____
_____
_____
_____
_____
_____

Conversations

DAY 28

The YESes I handled today:

_____
_____
_____
_____
_____
_____
_____

What I gained by saying YES:

_____
_____
_____
_____
_____
_____
_____

What were the dark and twisty parts of today's YESes?

_____
_____
_____
_____
_____
_____
_____

DAY 29

The YESes I handled today:

_____

_____

_____

_____

_____

_____

_____

What I gained by saying YES:

_____

_____

_____

_____

_____

_____

What were the dark and twisty parts of today's YESes?

_____

_____

_____

_____

_____

_____

Conversations

DAY 30

The YESes I handled today:

_____

_____

_____

_____

_____

_____

_____

What I gained by saying YES:

_____

_____

_____

_____

_____

_____

_____

What were the dark and twisty parts of today's YESes?

_____

_____

_____

_____

_____

_____

Conversations

DAY 31

The YESes I handled today:

_____

_____

_____

_____

_____

_____

_____

What I gained by saying YES:

_____

_____

_____

_____

_____

_____

_____

What were the dark and twisty parts of today's YESes?

_____

_____

_____

_____

_____

_____

_____

Dance

MONTH ELEVEN

YES TO DANCING IT OUT

Dance. *Dance*. Shake it left, shake it right,
groove everything you can groove. And don't you
dare care who is watching you. It's YOUR life.

Things I will say YES to this month:

_____

_____

_____

_____

_____

_____

_____

_____

_____

_____

_____

_____

_____

Dance

What is on your dance it out playlist?

_____
_____
_____
_____
_____
_____
_____
_____
_____
_____

Who is your dance it out partner?

_____
_____
_____
_____
_____
_____
_____
_____
_____
_____
_____

ALWAYS

DANCING

—— ✦ ——

in the

SUN.

—— ✦ —— ✦ ——

Dance

DAY 1

The YESes I handled today:

_____

_____

_____

_____

_____

_____

_____

What I gained by saying YES:

_____

_____

_____

_____

_____

_____

_____

What were the dark and twisty parts of today's YESes?

_____

_____

_____

_____

_____

_____

_____

Dance

DAY 2

The YESes I handled today:

_____
_____
_____
_____
_____
_____
_____

What I gained by saying YES:

_____
_____
_____
_____
_____
_____
_____

What were the dark and twisty parts of today's YESes?

_____
_____
_____
_____
_____
_____
_____

Dance

DAY 3

The YESes I handled today:

_____
_____
_____
_____
_____
_____
_____

What I gained by saying YES:

_____
_____
_____
_____
_____
_____
_____

What were the dark and twisty parts of today's YESes?

_____
_____
_____
_____
_____
_____
_____

Dance

DAY 4

The YESes I handled today:

_____

_____

_____

_____

_____

_____

_____

What I gained by saying YES:

_____

_____

_____

_____

_____

_____

What were the dark and twisty parts of today's YESes?

_____

_____

_____

_____

_____

_____

_____

Dance

DAY 5

The YESes I handled today:

_____

_____

_____

_____

_____

_____

_____

What I gained by saying YES:

_____

_____

_____

_____

_____

_____

_____

What were the dark and twisty parts of today's YESes?

_____

_____

_____

_____

_____

_____

_____

Dance

DAY 6

The YESes I handled today:

_____
_____
_____
_____
_____
_____
_____

What I gained by saying YES:

_____
_____
_____
_____
_____
_____
_____

What were the dark and twisty parts of today's YESes?

_____
_____
_____
_____
_____
_____

Dance

DAY 7

The YESes I handled today:

_____
_____
_____
_____
_____
_____
_____

What I gained by saying YES:

_____
_____
_____
_____
_____
_____
_____

What were the dark and twisty parts of today's YESes?

_____
_____
_____
_____
_____
_____
_____

Dance

DAY 8

The YESes I handled today:

_____

_____

_____

_____

_____

_____

What I gained by saying YES:

_____

_____

_____

_____

_____

_____

What were the dark and twisty parts of today's YESes?

_____

_____

_____

_____

_____

_____

Dance

DAY 9

The YESes I handled today:

_____
_____
_____
_____
_____
_____
_____

What I gained by saying YES:

_____
_____
_____
_____
_____
_____
_____

What were the dark and twisty parts of today's YESes?

_____
_____
_____
_____
_____
_____
_____

Dance

DAY 10

The YESes I handled today:

_____

_____

_____

_____

_____

_____

_____

What I gained by saying YES:

_____

_____

_____

_____

_____

_____

_____

What were the dark and twisty parts of today's YESes?

_____

_____

_____

_____

_____

_____

_____

Dance

DAY 11

The YESes I handled today:

_____

_____

_____

_____

_____

_____

_____

What I gained by saying YES:

_____

_____

_____

_____

_____

_____

_____

What were the dark and twisty parts of today's YESes?

_____

_____

_____

_____

_____

_____

_____

Dance

DAY 12

The YESes I handled today:

_____

_____

_____

_____

_____

_____

_____

What I gained by saying YES:

_____

_____

_____

_____

_____

_____

What were the dark and twisty parts of today's YESes?

_____

_____

_____

_____

_____

_____

Dance

DAY 13

The YESes I handled today:

_____
_____
_____
_____
_____
_____
_____

What I gained by saying YES:

_____
_____
_____
_____
_____
_____
_____

What were the dark and twisty parts of today's YESes?

_____
_____
_____
_____
_____
_____
_____

Dance

DAY 14

The YESes I handled today:

_____

_____

_____

_____

_____

_____

What I gained by saying YES:

_____

_____

_____

_____

_____

_____

What were the dark and twisty parts of today's YESes?

_____

_____

_____

_____

_____

_____

Dance

DAY 15

The YESes I handled today:

_____

_____

_____

_____

_____

_____

_____

What I gained by saying YES:

_____

_____

_____

_____

_____

_____

_____

What were the dark and twisty parts of today's YESes?

_____

_____

_____

_____

_____

_____

_____

THIS
DANCE

is a

CELEBRATION

of what

YOU

 can become.

Dance

DAY 16

The YESes I handled today:

_____

_____

_____

_____

_____

_____

What I gained by saying YES:

_____

_____

_____

_____

_____

_____

What were the dark and twisty parts of today's YESes?

_____

_____

_____

_____

_____

_____

Dance

DAY 17

The YESes I handled today:

_____

_____

_____

_____

_____

_____

_____

What I gained by saying YES:

_____

_____

_____

_____

_____

_____

What were the dark and twisty parts of today's YESes?

_____

_____

_____

_____

_____

_____

_____

Dance

DAY 18

The YESes I handled today:

_____

_____

_____

_____

_____

_____

What I gained by saying YES:

_____

_____

_____

_____

_____

_____

What were the dark and twisty parts of today's YESes?

_____

_____

_____

_____

_____

_____

Dance

DAY 19

The YESes I handled today:

_____
_____
_____
_____
_____
_____
_____

What I gained by saying YES:

_____
_____
_____
_____
_____
_____
_____

What were the dark and twisty parts of today's YESes?

_____
_____
_____
_____
_____
_____
_____

Dance

DAY 20

The YESes I handled today:

_____
_____
_____
_____
_____
_____
_____

What I gained by saying YES:

_____
_____
_____
_____
_____
_____
_____

What were the dark and twisty parts of today's YESes?

_____
_____
_____
_____
_____
_____
_____

Dance

DAY 21

The YESes I handled today:

_____

_____

_____

_____

_____

_____

_____

What I gained by saying YES:

_____

_____

_____

_____

_____

_____

_____

What were the dark and twisty parts of today's YESes?

_____

_____

_____

_____

_____

_____

_____

Dance

DAY 22

The YESes I handled today:

_____

_____

_____

_____

_____

_____

_____

What I gained by saying YES:

_____

_____

_____

_____

_____

_____

_____

What were the dark and twisty parts of today's YESes?

_____

_____

_____

_____

_____

_____

_____

Dance

DAY 23

The YESes I handled today:

_____
_____
_____
_____
_____
_____
_____

What I gained by saying YES:

_____
_____
_____
_____
_____
_____
_____

What were the dark and twisty parts of today's YESes?

_____
_____
_____
_____
_____
_____
_____

Dance

DAY 24

The YESes I handled today:

_____

_____

_____

_____

_____

_____

_____

What I gained by saying YES:

_____

_____

_____

_____

_____

_____

What were the dark and twisty parts of today's YESes?

_____

_____

_____

_____

_____

_____

Dance

DAY 25

The YESes I handled today:

_____

_____

_____

_____

_____

_____

_____

What I gained by saying YES:

_____

_____

_____

_____

_____

_____

_____

What were the dark and twisty parts of today's YESes?

_____

_____

_____

_____

_____

_____

_____

Dance

DAY 26

The YESes I handled today:

_____
_____
_____
_____
_____
_____
_____

What I gained by saying YES:

_____
_____
_____
_____
_____
_____
_____

What were the dark and twisty parts of today's YESes?

_____
_____
_____
_____
_____
_____
_____

Dance

DAY 27

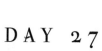

The YESes I handled today:

_____

_____

_____

_____

_____

_____

What I gained by saying YES:

_____

_____

_____

_____

_____

_____

What were the dark and twisty parts of today's YESes?

_____

_____

_____

_____

_____

_____

Dance

DAY 28

The YESes I handled today:

_____
_____
_____
_____
_____
_____
_____

What I gained by saying YES:

_____
_____
_____
_____
_____
_____
_____

What were the dark and twisty parts of today's YESes?

_____
_____
_____
_____
_____
_____
_____

Dance

DAY 29

The YESes I handled today:

_____

_____

_____

_____

_____

_____

_____

What I gained by saying YES:

_____

_____

_____

_____

_____

_____

_____

What were the dark and twisty parts of today's YESes?

_____

_____

_____

_____

_____

_____

_____

Dance

DAY 30

The YESes I handled today:

_____

_____

_____

_____

_____

_____

What I gained by saying YES:

_____

_____

_____

_____

_____

_____

What were the dark and twisty parts of today's YESes?

_____

_____

_____

_____

_____

_____

Dance

DAY 31

The YESes I handled today:

_____
_____
_____
_____
_____
_____
_____

What I gained by saying YES:

_____
_____
_____
_____
_____
_____

What were the dark and twisty parts of today's YESes?

_____
_____
_____
_____
_____
_____
_____

Me

MONTH TWELVE

YES TO WHO I AM

Like all the best stories, you are unfolding exactly
as you should. Trust that there are no rules or paths
that must be followed if they feel untrue to you.

Things I will say YES to this month:

_____

_____

_____

_____

_____

_____

_____

_____

_____

_____

_____

_____

_____

Me

Who do people expect you to be?

_____

_____

_____

_____

_____

_____

_____

_____

_____

_____

Now, wipe the slate clean. Write your own happy ending:

_____

_____

_____

_____

_____

_____

_____

_____

_____

_____

WHAT

AM I AFRAID

they will see if

I AM REALLY

MYSELF?

DAY 1

The YESes I handled today:

_____
_____
_____
_____
_____
_____
_____

What I gained by saying YES:

_____
_____
_____
_____
_____
_____
_____

What were the dark and twisty parts of today's YESes?

_____
_____
_____
_____
_____
_____
_____

Me

DAY 2

The YESes I handled today:

_____
_____
_____
_____
_____
_____
_____
_____

What I gained by saying YES:

_____
_____
_____
_____
_____
_____
_____
_____

What were the dark and twisty parts of today's YESes?

_____
_____
_____
_____
_____
_____
_____

Me

DAY 3

The YESes I handled today:

_____
_____
_____
_____
_____
_____
_____

What I gained by saying YES:

_____
_____
_____
_____
_____
_____
_____

What were the dark and twisty parts of today's YESes?

_____
_____
_____
_____
_____
_____
_____

DAY 4

The YESes I handled today:

_____

_____

_____

_____

_____

_____

_____

What I gained by saying YES:

_____

_____

_____

_____

_____

_____

_____

What were the dark and twisty parts of today's YESes?

_____

_____

_____

_____

_____

_____

_____

Me

DAY 5

The YESes I handled today:

_____
_____
_____
_____
_____
_____
_____

What I gained by saying YES:

_____
_____
_____
_____
_____
_____

What were the dark and twisty parts of today's YESes?

_____
_____
_____
_____
_____
_____

DAY 6

The YESes I handled today:

_____
_____
_____
_____
_____
_____

What I gained by saying YES:

_____
_____
_____
_____
_____
_____

What were the dark and twisty parts of today's YESes?

_____
_____
_____
_____
_____
_____

Me

DAY 7

The YESes I handled today:

_____
_____
_____
_____
_____
_____
_____

What I gained by saying YES:

_____
_____
_____
_____
_____
_____
_____

What were the dark and twisty parts of today's YESes?

_____
_____
_____
_____
_____
_____
_____

Me

DAY 8

The YESes I handled today:

_____

_____

_____

_____

_____

_____

What I gained by saying YES:

_____

_____

_____

_____

_____

_____

What were the dark and twisty parts of today's YESes?

_____

_____

_____

_____

_____

_____

Me

DAY 9

The YESes I handled today:

_____
_____
_____
_____
_____
_____
_____

What I gained by saying YES:

_____
_____
_____
_____
_____
_____
_____

What were the dark and twisty parts of today's YESes?

_____
_____
_____
_____
_____
_____
_____

Me

DAY 10

The YESes I handled today:

_____
_____
_____
_____
_____
_____
_____

What I gained by saying YES:

_____
_____
_____
_____
_____
_____
_____

What were the dark and twisty parts of today's YESes?

_____
_____
_____
_____
_____
_____
_____

Me

DAY 11

The YESes I handled today:

_____

_____

_____

_____

_____

_____

What I gained by saying YES:

_____

_____

_____

_____

_____

_____

What were the dark and twisty parts of today's YESes?

_____

_____

_____

_____

_____

_____

Me

DAY 12

The YESes I handled today:

_____
_____
_____
_____
_____
_____

What I gained by saying YES:

_____
_____
_____
_____
_____
_____

What were the dark and twisty parts of today's YESes?

_____
_____
_____
_____
_____
_____

Me

DAY 13

The YESes I handled today:

_____

_____

_____

_____

_____

_____

_____

What I gained by saying YES:

_____

_____

_____

_____

_____

_____

_____

What were the dark and twisty parts of today's YESes?

_____

_____

_____

_____

_____

_____

_____

Me

DAY 14

The YESes I handled today:

_____

_____

_____

_____

_____

_____

What I gained by saying YES:

_____

_____

_____

_____

_____

_____

What were the dark and twisty parts of today's YESes?

_____

_____

_____

_____

_____

_____

THE
RULE

is

THERE

 are

NO RULES.

Me

DAY 15

The YESes I handled today:

_____
_____
_____
_____
_____
_____
_____

What I gained by saying YES:

_____
_____
_____
_____
_____
_____
_____

What were the dark and twisty parts of today's YESes?

_____
_____
_____
_____
_____
_____
_____

DAY 16

The YESes I handled today:

_____

_____

_____

_____

_____

_____

What I gained by saying YES:

_____

_____

_____

_____

_____

_____

What were the dark and twisty parts of today's YESes?

_____

_____

_____

_____

_____

_____

DAY 17

The YESes I handled today:

_____
_____
_____
_____
_____
_____
_____

What I gained by saying YES:

_____
_____
_____
_____
_____
_____
_____

What were the dark and twisty parts of today's YESes?

_____
_____
_____
_____
_____
_____
_____

Me

DAY 18

The YESes I handled today:

_____
_____
_____
_____
_____
_____
_____

What I gained by saying YES:

_____
_____
_____
_____
_____
_____
_____

What were the dark and twisty parts of today's YESes?

_____
_____
_____
_____
_____
_____
_____

Me

DAY 19

The YESes I handled today:

_____
_____
_____
_____
_____
_____
_____

What I gained by saying YES:

_____
_____
_____
_____
_____
_____
_____

What were the dark and twisty parts of today's YESes?

_____
_____
_____
_____
_____
_____
_____

I am

DIFFERENT.

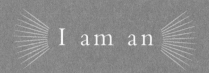

I am an

ORIGINAL.

And like everyone else,

I AM

HERE

to take up space in the universe.

I DO SO

WITH PRIDE.

Me

DAY 20

The YESes I handled today:

_____

_____

_____

_____

_____

_____

_____

What I gained by saying YES:

_____

_____

_____

_____

_____

_____

_____

What were the dark and twisty parts of today's YESes?

_____

_____

_____

_____

_____

_____

_____

Me

DAY 21

The YESes I handled today:

_____
_____
_____
_____
_____
_____
_____

What I gained by saying YES:

_____
_____
_____
_____
_____
_____
_____

What were the dark and twisty parts of today's YESes?

_____
_____
_____
_____
_____
_____
_____

DAY 22

The YESes I handled today:

_____

_____

_____

_____

_____

_____

_____

What I gained by saying YES:

_____

_____

_____

_____

_____

_____

_____

What were the dark and twisty parts of today's YESes?

_____

_____

_____

_____

_____

_____

_____

DAY 23

The YESes I handled today:

_____
_____
_____
_____
_____
_____
_____

What I gained by saying YES:

_____
_____
_____
_____
_____
_____
_____

What were the dark and twisty parts of today's YESes?

_____
_____
_____
_____
_____
_____
_____

Me

DAY 24

The YESes I handled today:

_____

_____

_____

_____

_____

_____

_____

What I gained by saying YES:

_____

_____

_____

_____

_____

_____

_____

What were the dark and twisty parts of today's YESes?

_____

_____

_____

_____

_____

_____

_____

Me

DAY 25

The YESes I handled today:

_____
_____
_____
_____
_____
_____
_____

What I gained by saying YES:

_____
_____
_____
_____
_____
_____
_____

What were the dark and twisty parts of today's YESes?

_____
_____
_____
_____
_____
_____
_____

HAPPINESS

comes from being who

YOU
ACTUALLY
ARE

instead of who you think

YOU ARE
SUPPOSED
TO BE.

Me

DAY 26

The YESes I handled today:

_____

_____

_____

_____

_____

_____

What I gained by saying YES:

_____

_____

_____

_____

_____

_____

What were the dark and twisty parts of today's YESes?

_____

_____

_____

_____

_____

_____

_____

DAY 27

The YESes I handled today:

_____
_____
_____
_____
_____
_____
_____

What I gained by saying YES:

_____
_____
_____
_____
_____
_____
_____

What were the dark and twisty parts of today's YESes?

_____
_____
_____
_____
_____
_____
_____

Me

DAY 28

The YESes I handled today:

_____
_____
_____
_____
_____
_____
_____

What I gained by saying YES:

_____
_____
_____
_____
_____
_____
_____

What were the dark and twisty parts of today's YESes?

_____
_____
_____
_____
_____
_____
_____

DAY 29

The YESes I handled today:

_____

_____

_____

_____

_____

_____

_____

What I gained by saying YES:

_____

_____

_____

_____

_____

_____

_____

What were the dark and twisty parts of today's YESes?

_____

_____

_____

_____

_____

_____

DAY 30

The YESes I handled today:

_____
_____
_____
_____
_____
_____
_____

What I gained by saying YES:

_____
_____
_____
_____
_____
_____
_____

What were the dark and twisty parts of today's YESes?

_____
_____
_____
_____
_____
_____
_____

Me

DAY 31

The YESes I handled today:

_____

_____

_____

_____

_____

_____

What I gained by saying YES:

_____

_____

_____

_____

_____

_____

What were the dark and twisty parts of today's YESes?

_____

_____

_____

_____

_____

_____

BE

◇ ◇ ◇ your own ◇ ◇ ◇

NARRATOR,

—— and go for a ——

HAPPY

ENDING.

YOUR YEAR OF YES

Who are you after your Year of Yes?

_____
_____
_____
_____
_____
_____
_____
_____
_____
_____
_____
_____
_____
_____
_____
_____
_____
_____
_____
_____
_____
_____
_____
_____
_____

What do you want to share from your Year of Yes with somebody else?

_____
_____
_____
_____
_____
_____
_____
_____
_____
_____
_____
_____
_____
_____
_____
_____
_____
_____
_____
_____
_____
_____
_____
_____
_____
_____

What's next? Who do you want to become after your Year of Yes?

_____

_____

_____

_____

_____

_____

_____

_____

_____

_____

_____

_____

_____

_____

_____

_____

_____

_____

_____

_____

_____

_____

_____

_____

_____

ABOUT THE AUTHOR

SHONDA RHIMES is the critically acclaimed and award-winning creator and executive producer of the hit television series *Grey's Anatomy, Private Practice* and *Scandal* and the executive producer of *How to Get Away with Murder* and *The Catch*. Rhimes holds a BA in English Literature with Creative Writing from Dartmouth College and received her MFA from the USC School of Cinema-Television. Born and raised in Chicago, Illinois, Rhimes now lives in Shondaland, a very real and very imagined place that could be somewhere inside Los Angeles. She's the proud mother of three daughters.